KEYWORDS IN LANGUAGE AND LITERACY

'We've got to produce people who can write proper English.
. . . You cannot educate people properly unless you do it on a
basic framework and drilling system.'

HRH the Prince of Wales

'Language is indissolubly linked to power. . . . To think
seriously about teaching English . . . we need to understand
the paradox that language is both potentially liberating and
potentially enslaving.'

Harold Rosen

The teaching and practice of language and literacy is a hotly
contested subject. Questions like 'what is standard English?',
'what is grammar?' and the place accorded to canonical writers
in the curriculum continue to provoke controversy. In this
handy A to Z guide to language and literacy Ronald Carter
unpicks the meaning of key terms like 'grammar', 'proper
English', 'real books', 'text' and 'discourse', and the way in
which such concepts are used – and abused – by teachers,
politicians, linguists, journalists and employers.

Each concise definition is cross-referenced and supported by
extensive examples and references to further reading. Designed
as a dictionary, but possessing an encyclopaedic range, *Keywords
in Language and Literacy* provides an invaluable guide to the
debates surrounding language and literacy. An indispensable
book for all teachers and students of language and education,
and anyone interested in the place of language in our schools.

Ronald Carter is Professor of Modern English Language and
Head of Department of English Studies at the University of
Nottingham. He was National Director of the Language
in the National Curriculum project from 1989–1992 and is
currently editor of the Routledge Interface Series in Language
and Literary Studies.

KEYWORDS IN LANGUAGE AND LITERACY

Ronald Carter

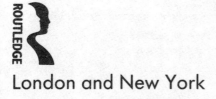

London and New York

First published 1995
by Routledge
11 New Fetter Lane, London EC4P 4EE

Simultaneously published in the USA and Canada
by Routledge
29 West 35th Street, New York, NY 10001

© 1995 Ronald Carter

Typeset in Bembo by Florencetype Ltd, Stoodleigh, Devon

Printed and bound in Great Britain by
Clays Ltd, St Ives plc

British Library Cataloguing in Publication Data
A catalogue record for this book is available from the British Library

Library of Congress Cataloguing in Publication Data
A catalogue record for this book has been requested

ISBN 0–415–11928–6 (hbk)
ISBN 0–415–11929–4 (pbk)

. . . the way in which education is organised can be seen to express, consciously and unconsciously, the wider organisation of a society, so that what has been thought of as a 'simple distribution' is in fact an active shaping to particular social ends.

Raymond Williams, The Long Revolution
(Penguin, Harmondsworth, 1965)

Language is a system of sounds, meanings and structures with which we make sense of the world around us. It functions as a tool of thought; as a means of social organisation; as the repository and means of transmission of knowledge; as the raw material of literature, and as the creator and sustainer – or destroyer – of human relationships. It changes inevitably over time and, as change is not uniform, from place to place. Because language is a fundamental part of being human, it is an important aspect of a person's sense of self; because it is a fundamental feature of any community, it is an important aspect of a person's sense of social identity.

The Cox Report (DES, 1989, para. 6.18)

Children will never learn to speak and write properly if, for instance, their teachers tell them that 'we was' is as 'valid' as 'we were'. A study commissioned by the government on how English should be taught under the national curriculum summed up many teachers' views. The government refused to publish it because it disagreed with the findings. It is not hard to see why. To regard grammar in terms of mistakes, the report recommended, was 'unhelpful'. Rather, grammar should be seen as 'a series of options'.

Grammar is not a series of options. There is correct standard English and there is bad English. If children want to use slang in the street, then fine – but only if they know better. If they want to improve themselves, they need to know how to speak and write properly when the occasion requires . . . What hope has an unemployed teenager of finding a job if he cannot fill in a form correctly or write a grammatical letter? The report suppressed by the government claimed that 'he ain't done it' and 'she come here yesterday' are 'no more a barrier to achievement'.

The Times, editorial, 22 April 1992

Every time the question of the language surfaces, in one way or another, it means that a series of other problems are coming to the fore: the formation and enlargement of the governing class, the need to establish more intimate and secure relationships between the governing groups and the national-popular mass, in other words to reorganise the cultural hegemony.

Antonio Gramsci, *Selections from Cultural Writings*, ed. D. Forgacs and G. Nowell-Smith (Lawrence & Wishart, London, 1985)

Let them leave language to their lonely betters
Who count some days and long for certain letters;
We, too, make noises when we laugh or weep:
Words are for those with promises to keep.

W. H. Auden, 'Their Lonely Betters', in *Collected Shorter Poems* (Faber, London, 1966)

CONTENTS

vii

PREFACE AND ACKNOWLEDGEMENTS

The teaching and practice of literacy has again become a highly contested area in the 1990s, with disputes among professionals and interventions by governments creating ideological battle-grounds which have serious repercussions for the formation of the curriculum.

The main aim of this book is to introduce some central concepts in the teaching and practice of literacy in English by examining in particular key words and terms used to describe literacy practices. The book is designed as an A–Z of such key words and many of the entries begin by an unpacking of linguistic ideas or of the assumptions about language which underpin such ideas. Language use is therefore often a starting point for definition and description.

The book also shows the extent to which descriptive linguistics, and especially sociolinguistics, can illuminate the relationship between language and literacy and can contribute to an understanding of the social and cultural discourses that condition how issues of language and literacy are debated. The book is designed for students of education, in-service and pre-service teachers and for all those with an interest in the relationship between language and literacy.

Any dictionary of words and terms is inevitably highly selective; indeed, it is especially characteristic of debates at the interface of language and literacy that there will be considered to be omissions from any list of key words such as this, and that certain topics will be considered to be treated either in insufficient detail or in too great a degree of detail.

Certainly, there are words which have proved central to literacy debates in Britain. One such word is 'expert', a term of disparagement of the professional teacher or teacher educator in language and literacy (unless the expert represents an acceptable point of view) and widely used in the discourses of politicians and certain sections of the British press; another is the word 'discipline' which slips in the meanings constructed for it from that of an almost military code of behaviour (felt by 'traditionalists' to be lacking in schools) to that of a subject 'discipline' such as English (which, for many sections of the press and for government ministers in Britain, is not a subject because 'trendy' teaching methods do not foster appropriately disciplined approaches to learning). It will be seen, too, how similar inflections for 'progressive' and 'trendy', 'orthodox' and 'traditional' could be explored. For example, 'traditional' is rarely exemplified, perhaps because its primary association is with a nostalgia for some previous 'golden age' in which teaching and learning English was an ordered, uniform process. (Wherever possible, however, terms which have specifically linguistic roots or outcomes are the starting points for definitions and descriptions.)

In one sense this may be a timely book since, as the quotation from Gramsci on the foregoing page of extracts illustrates, issues of language appear to come to the fore at moments of national crisis. It is perhaps therefore no accident that the issue of standard and proper English should surface again in the late 1980s and early 1990s since those years encompass a historical shift in the identity of the country which has been given a particular impetus by the question of the extent to which Britain properly belongs inside Europe. They are years in which the question of what it is to be British is at the centre of national consciousness. They are also years in which forces of centralisation, manifested in particular in centralised educational planning through a national curriculum, were gathered in part at least to counter what was perceived by a Conservative government to be the threat of local, regional, multilingual and multicultural fragmentation. An insistence on a homogenous, codified and unifying standard English becomes in such a context an index of order in a world of increasing diversity and 'disorder' from which traditional (Victorian) moral and social values appear to have departed.

In this respect this whole book illustrates what Mikhail Bakhtin (1981) calls the centripetal and centrifugal forces in language and society. Centripetal forces in language push towards a unitary language system and cultural and political centralisation. The centrifugal forces work against the centripetal forces and push towards variation, diversity and disunification. Bakhtin points out that it is this opposition which keeps language alive but that both forces are always detectable, as many of the entries in this book indicate, even though at particular moments in history one or the other may appear to be in the ascendant.

This book has been put together over a number of years and has been influenced by books and people too numerous to mention. Raymond Williams's *Keywords*, though more explicitly an exercise in socio-historical semantics, is an obvious source of inspiration. My work on the LINC (Language in the National Curriculum) project has also served to sharpen understanding of a number of words which were endlessly recycled during the life of that project. Though I owe a particular debt of understanding to the many colleagues, especially the regional coordinators with whom I had the pleasure of working during that time, particular thanks must go to Rebecca Bunting and John Richmond for comments on parts of this manuscript, to John Richmond for allowing me to use material which was jointly written and to John Harris and Jeff Wilkinson who worked with me on a LINC glossary on which I have, in places, drawn for the purpose of this book. The success of the LINC project with teachers and its lasting contribution to their understanding of language is proportionate to the British government's disapproval of the project. In this limited respect, the book is therefore a testimony to the LINC project and to the competing discourses which it and similar projects continue to generate.

Ronald Carter
Nottingham, May 1994

accent

Glottal stops ain't allowed no more

The latest suggestion that schoolchildren should speak
Standard English – even in the playground's rough and
tumble – has generally been received as a good thing by the
world of adults.

From the age of five, the nation's children may now be
encouraged to pick up their aitches and drop the ubiqui-
tous glottal stops, *ain'ts* and other manifestations of non–U
grammar. With regional accents allowed to remain, the
result is likely to be that BBC English is once again a
model for the nation.

(*Times Educational Supplement*, 25 September 1992)

The term 'accent' refers to those features of pronunciation
which identify a person either geographically or socially. A
geographical accent can be associated with a specific town or
city (e.g. Liverpool, New York) or a particular region (e.g.
Texas) or with national groups speaking the same language
(e.g. Australian). It can also show whether a speaker is a
native speaker of a language. For example, 'She speaks French
with an English accent.'

Social accents relate more to social and educational background. An example of this in Britain is *Received Pronunciation* (RP), commonly known as 'BBC', 'posh', or 'Oxford' English. This is a geographically neutral accent in so far as speakers using it do not betray their geographical origins. It is, however, often associated with public schools and professional uses and tends to be a local accent in several parts of southern England, especially in areas surrounding London. Because of its geographical neutrality, it is popularly but wrongly thought that people speaking in RP have no accent. In terms of a linguistic description of accent, everyone has an accent, which may be geographical or social or both and vary according to the speaker's situation.

RP is the model of pronunciation which figures prominently in courses for the teaching of English as a foreign or second language and is the preferred model in a number of countries overseas. Increasingly, however, the model is seen as simply one of many national accents, and other native-speaker accents, such as Australian and American English, are being taught in contexts where it had previously been assumed that there was only one correct form of pronunciation. The choice of pronunciation model, as well as the variety of international English taught, is also an ideological choice. Language learners in several countries pride themselves on the greater sense of national identity conferred by speaking English with an Indian or a Nigerian or a Singaporean accent.

The sociolinguistic situation in Britain regarding accent variation is not dissimilar. An RP accent may be geographically neutral but it has a marked social significance, being associated, in particular, with its normally more upper-class speakers. Much sociolinguistic research (e.g. Trudgill, 1983, 1984) has underlined the extent to which speakers either aspire or at least orient to an RP accent in most formal contexts of language use, such as answering the telephone or in interviews. The phenomenon of hypercorrection neatly illustrates this point. Hypercorrection is the tendency to over-correct low-prestige vowels with high-prestige vowels even when they are not needed. It leads to the conversion of standard English words such as plastic into 'plarstic'. It leads to people fearful of nuclear emissions convinced that not even a gas-mask but a new kind of 'gars-mask' will be needed.

Advertisers are, as always, linguistically sensitive to such phenomena. For example, the accents used to overlay many current television and radio advertisements betray some fundamental British social attitudes towards accent variation. Thus, a Standard English accent (predominantly received pronunciation) is used to sell banking and insurance policies, lean cuisine ready meals, expensive liqueurs and exotic holidays; regional accents are used to market beers, especially cider, holidays in inclement British coastal resorts and wholesome foods such as 'bootiful' turkeys from Norfolk and wholemeal bread which is either ''ot from t'oven' or 'wi' nowt teken out'. Given the connection between Standard English, 'proper accents', purity and cleanliness it may not be surprising to learn that in Britain bleach is marketed in RP accents. Dialects may coexist with the marketing of washing powders but hardly ever with the marketing of the more deeply cleansing properties of bleach.

In the teaching of National Curriculum English in British schools strong emphasis is placed on Standard English and on the clear and comprehensible use of Standard English in writing and in speech. Because of the clear connection of Standard English (as a prestige variety of English) with RP (as a prestige accent of English), it is, however, but a short step from correction of writing of pupils' non-standard dialects to correction of pupils' non-standard accents. Research evidence underlines that overcorrection of the speech of very young children can result in a low self-image, lack of confidence and linguistic confusion during crucial years of language development.

Even though it is widely recognised that Standard English can be spoken with any accent, for example, that standard English spoken in a Scots accent or a Lancashire accent is still Standard English, the notion that there are rules of 'pure' pronunciation and a single correct accent is not easily eroded. The situation is not helped by the existence, as noted above, of RP as an accent which has considerable international currency. A balanced view is one which recognises the importance of the need to preserve self-confidence and a sense of linguistic identity alongside the facilitating of clear communication. The difficulties in achieving this balance are neatly illustrated, however, by the quotation from the *Times Educational Supplement* which is at the head of this entry. Apart from a basic confusion between accent (matter of pronunciation such as 'aitches' and 'glottal stops') and grammar ('ain't'), the statement can be further confusing for teachers for whom it is written by suggesting a more rigid opposition between standard and non-standard Englishes than is either desirable or is matched by the linguistic reality of contemporary Britain.

See also **dialect, proper, purism**
Further reading   Coggle, 1993; Honey, 1989; Trudgill, 1975

applied linguistics   Applied linguistics is the application of linguistic theories, descriptions and methods to the solution of language problems which have arisen in a range of human, cultural and social contexts. One of its main uses is in the exploration of problems in language learning and teaching and, for many, the term is used with almost exclusive reference to this field. However, the term 'applied linguistics' is used in relation to other fields, such as: literary studies (stylistics); translation studies; lexicography; language planning; as well as being specific to other 'applied' branches of linguistics such as clinical linguistics and critical linguistics. Ideally, applied linguists should work alongside other professionals in the exploration of language problems or difficulties so that the applications of linguistics are the result of a genuine synthesis rather than one in which answers are found only according to an agenda provided by the linguist.

See also **educational linguistics, stylistics**
Further reading Carter, 1993; Hasan and Williams (eds), forthcoming; Richards *et al.*, 1993; Widdowson, 1989

appropriate In many public discussions the term 'appropriate' is opposed to the term 'correct'. Appropriateness or appropriacy is a sociolinguistic concept which stresses that language varies according to the social context in which it is used. The term is used to describe any variety or forms of language which are judged to be suitable or possible within a particular situation. Thus, contracted forms such as 'I would've' or elisions such as 'I wanna' are appropriate in most contexts of informal speech, in some informal written contexts and for the representation of informal speech in writing. More prescriptive accounts of language consider the notion of appropriacy to be unduly relativistic, preferring to regard particular language forms as correct or incorrect irrespective of the social situation.

See also **proper**
Further reading Trudgill, 1984

author(ship) The concept of authorship is central to romantic philosophies of English teaching. Within such philosophies what is imaginative and literary about language, which stems from the creative unconscious of an individual author, is also, in turn, central. Authors express personal, individual visions which are uniquely theirs. Whereas in some pre-industrial cultures creativity is collective and the production of literary works often anonymous, romantic conceptions of creativity arise in part in opposition to a perceived impersonality in industrialised cultures and assert the originality of the individual voice.

As far as literacy practices are concerned, such privileging of the individual author and of unconscious and mysterious creative processes results in high value being placed both on the study of literary texts and on creative writing. Such an emphasis can also produce assumptions that appreciation of literature is best intuited rather than too explicitly taught and that genuinely creative writing cannot be taught. Consequently, the craft of writing is not prioritised, the writing of personal narratives is preferred to impersonal reports and writers are encouraged to find their own unique 'voice' as writers. Correspondingly, too, the human voice is associated with speech which is in turn assumed to be a more natural, personal, spontaneous, truthful and less contrived form of language. The most successfully authored texts are then those which most closely approximate the spoken language. Such a philosophy applied to language development results in relatively restricted genres of writing and a rather limited view of writing development. For example, writing for the world of work outside school often needs to be impersonal and instrumental, with the personal voice of the individual author reduced.

Advocates of the central importance of authorship to English teaching stress, however, that learning is at its most effective, especially in processes of writing, when writing is not a blind transcription of existing forms and content but when an individual imprint is placed on the writing. Writing to learn through recording unique experience is a key element in learning to write. A number of specific examples relevant to this entry and including texts written by children can be found in the entry for **genre**.

See also **genre, literary language, literature, narrative, personal growth, romantics and reactionaries**
Further reading Gilbert, 1989,1990; Graves, 1983; Luke, 1988

B

'back to basics'   The school curriculum for English in many English-speaking countries has had three main features: its diversity, its potential for development and renewal, and its being continually subject to public criticism, particularly over alleged declines in standards of language use.

In Britain, in the period prior to the 1960s, mother-tongue English teaching was characterised by an emphasis on explicit teaching about the formal properties of the language, together with an approach to texts which emphasised the importance of comprehension of words and phrases. In the 1960s and 1970s greater emphasis was placed on pupil-centred approaches to learning and on the development of the individuality and creativity of the pupil. This involved a rejection of formal language exercises and a promotion of the discovery – through writing, talk and reading – of an individual voice and of a response to texts. Responses to literary texts were judged to be central to this development of 'personal growth' and the curriculum became largely one in which personal expression and the appropriate use of language according to context took precedence over exercises in correct usage.

One of the most powerful statements of this commitment to a diverse and broad view of English exists in the Bullock Report (DES, 1975), a major report by a government-appointed committee on the teaching of English as a

7

mother tongue. The Bullock Committee rejected a return to the language teaching practices of the past but, among its many recommendations, advocated a higher level of awareness of the properties and functions of language on the part of teachers, particularly in their preparation and in-service training. The report had received an enthusiastic reception from the English teaching profession but received some public criticism for not advocating a concentration on basic skills of literacy taught by formal methods of language training.

The 1980s witnessed an extended debate about education in the basic skills, particularly basic skills of literacy and numeracy. Such a debate has been by no means confined to Britain, and has been conducted in parallel ways in a number of other countries of the world. The debate has, however, been a public one, at least in Britain, and has attracted a high level of media interest, some of which is illustrated in this book.

As far as English teaching is concerned there has been a particularly public focus on language, and on basic language skills of grammar, spelling and punctuation and neatness of handwriting. At the level of public debate in Britain much government and media comment has stressed, above all, the need for a return to more formalistic approaches to English teaching with a concentration on the need to teach standard spoken and written English to all pupils, and to teach the rules of standard English grammar. Although outside professional circles the word 'grammar' is used as a kind of hold-all for 'good' or 'correct' English, there has been within the English teaching profession an extended parallel debate about the role of explicit knowledge about language (including grammatical organisation) and a general conclusion has been reached that there is a need for teachers and pupils to have a greater understanding of the workings of the language. 'Back to basics' also involves an emphasis on basic reading skills, particularly on phonics approaches to reading and on writing which prioritises accuracy in the secretarial aspects of language use.

There remain, however, disagreements among teachers concerning the most appropriate ways to respond to government requirements for a more language–centred English curriculum and for a greater concentration on 'standards' of English usage. There is above all strong resistance on the part of many English teachers to any return to the teaching of grammar as practised prior to the 1960s. Such teaching was characterised by analysis of clauses into component parts (mainly as analytical drills) and was often accompanied by teaching by means of decontextualised exercises. These practices were abandoned in the early 1960s. Calls against 'back to basics' and a return to grammar teaching regularly cite research findings by English teaching professionals which deny any connection between improved language competence and an explicit teaching of grammar. Such moves would, it has been argued throughout the 1980s, also reverse the main methodological advances of the previous twenty-five years.

Two key documents entitled *English 5 to 16: Curriculum Matters* (1 and 2) provoked a questioning in Britain during the 1980s of the need for a 'back to basics' movement. These documents gave a significant impetus to the debate on the particular nuances of meaning 'English' should have in the curriculum in Britain, but are in themselves insufficiently substantial to justify the kind of extended treatment given below to the Kingman and Cox Committee reports. *English 5 to 16: Curriculum Matters 1* (1984) was published in 1984 by the Department of Education and Science. It was essentially a discussion document prepared by HMI (Her Majesty's government school inspectors) in order to stimulate debate about English teaching in the 1980s and beyond.

One proposal in *Curriculum Matters 1* was for pupils to be taught more directly about the English language, particularly its forms and structures. It was seized on by many English teachers as being particularly retrogressive and as representing a reversion to the kinds of pedagogic and curricular practices which had been firmly rejected by the profession in the early 1960s. The debate generated by *Curriculum matters 1* was vigorous and committed and the government inspectorate undertook to record and respond to the arguments

9

presented to it. The republication of the document in the form of *Curriculum Matters 2* constitutes a kind of barometer of beliefs in what constitutes good practice in English teaching. *English 5 to 16: Curriculum Matters 2* (DES, 1986) contains 'Responses to curriculum matters 1' and is a rather more guarded document. It clearly acknowledges the strength of reaction against some of the positions adopted in the previous document. One of the main conclusions reached was that a committee of inquiry be set up to investigate further the possibilities for providing pupils (and teachers) with greater knowledge of the workings of the English language. The outcome was the publication of the Kingman Report by the Kingman Committee.

This entry has concentrated on 'back to basics' in language and language teaching but the same impetus affects the teaching of literature, with calls for a return to the compulsory teaching of Shakespeare and classical, canonical writers. There is also a further connection between a basic English curriculum and a return to basic, pre-twentieth-century moral and social values.

See also **canon, drills, grammar, Kingman, personal growth, Shakespeare**
Further reading DES, 1989; Marenbon, 1987

bidialectalism Individuals who are bidialectal are able to use more than one dialect of a language and know how and when to switch between these different codes. Normally, this ability includes a competence in using both a standard and a non-standard dialect. The term is also used to describe a particular educational policy according to which pupils who are not native-speaking users of a standard dialect are encouraged to acquire that dialect. At the same time pedagogies are developed to support the non-standard dialects and the pupil's competence in appropriate code-switching between the two dialects.

See also **creole, dialect**
Further reading Trudgill, 1975, 1983

bilingualism A bilingual is a person who has mastered the essential skills of writing, reading and speaking in two languages, although in most cases one language is known better than the other. The term 'bilingualism' is also used in connection with individuals who are trilingual or quadrilingual, normally reserving the term multilingualism for use with nations or societies. It is likely that the languages will be used in different situations; for example, one language might be used at work, while the other might be used in the home. Bilinguals also code-switch between languages according to whom they are talking, according to the subject matter and according to the relative formality of the situation. Not all bilinguals are bicultural; that is, they may be able to speak two or more languages but may only know how to behave according to values associated with the communities speaking one of the languages.

Bilingualism and multilingualism are central to national language planning. Their existence within a national languages profile may be judged either to be a problem or a resource depending on the attitudes adopted by the state to the existence of speakers of more than one language. In the case of socieities that view bilingualism as a problem rather than as a resource it is worth remembering that there are more countries in the world where bilingualism is the norm and monolingualism a problem.

See also **bidialectalism, culture, language planning, multilingualism**
Further reading Bourne 1989; Miller, 1983

Black English

We need to look at the productive skills of speakers

(and writers) in terms of a strategic accomplishment in performance and not in terms of a deficit or inadequacy in competence. It is impossible to define what constitutes the minimal competence one must have to be adequate except relative to the norms of a particular community . . . It will mean at the same time recognising students' rights to their own language.

(Romaine, 1984: 251–2)

Black British people of Caribbean origin have a strong sense of language choices to be made. In each Caribbean nation there is a variety of language present which includes one or more creoles and the standard form of the official language. The extent to which individual speakers can, or choose to, use that range depends on their social and economic status or aspirations, on the level of their education, and on how far they keep contact with their roots. At any particular moment, the choice of language people make from the range depends on who they are, whom they are speaking to, where and for what purpose. Nor is it as simple as to say that a speaker chooses from only two options: creole or the standard language. There is a repertoire of usage available, from full creole through to something close to the standard language with a few creole features.

Some older people of Caribbean origin living in Britain are likely to remember the sharp distinction made between the language appropriate for schooling and the language they used at home and with friends out of school. Depending on individual experience, they may have learnt to make the daily shift with no difficulty or embarrassment; many did. On the other hand, it may have been a matter of conflict and tension, particularly if the school encouraged the idea that creole was 'bad talk' , and reprimanded or even punished children using it in school. This attitude could have an effect on the home, too, if parents accepted and reinforced the idea that creole was limited or subversive or bad, and that their children would be better off abandoning it.

The sense of a repertoire is more likely to be part of the

understanding of language of many British children of Caribbean origin today. But other factors intervene too. One is that black British children will have taken on the local – nearly always urban – accent and dialect of the place where they live. Another is that some young black people have readopted a form of Caribbean creole as a badge of their culture, of solidarity with their peers – a solidarity which includes conscious resistance to racism. This form is closest to Jamaican creole and has been called British Jamaican or British Black English. So – depending again on individual experience, on attitudes learnt at home or with peers, and on age – black children and young people may have access to:

- Standard English;
- a local indigenous accent and dialect;
- the accent and dialect of a Caribbean creole learnt from older people in their family;
- and a language which is a conscious expression of the identity of black youth.

(The third and fourth of these will be very similar – not identical – if the young person's origins are in Jamaica; they will be distinct if their origins are elsewhere in the Caribbean). A striking proof of the significance of British black English as a unifying force is the fact that some young black people with no connections at all in the Caribbean – with a background in an African country, for example – can be heard speaking it.

As ever with language, these languages and varieties of language will interact in the speaker's total competence; the speaker will switch, slide and mix between them, depending on the situation. It is a complex and dynamic picture. Here is an example of a piece of writing by a year 9 pupil which shows the influence of varieties of British Black English:

At the Night Club
One night I was invited to a night club with some of my friends. At 11.00 I got ready to go to the night club. My friends boyfriend pick me up. We got to the night club at 11.30. My friends boyfriend pour me a glass of sherry

and left me all by myself. I stood around doing nothing, no one ask me for a dance I got so board that I went outside to get some fresh air and came back in. Later on I went to the changing room to get ready to go home. I open the changing room door and I left it open. Then suddenly the door slammed so hard that it frightened the life out of me . . .

Pat, year 9

The example shows the influence of the Jamaican creole use of the unmarked form of verbs like 'pick', 'pour', 'ask', 'open' in the past tense (SE requires an 'ed' ending). But Pat also uses Standard forms in 'slammed' and 'frightened', and always uses the Standard forms, as in 'got', 'left', 'stood', 'went', when the past tense is formed by changing the stem of the verb rather than by adding 'ed'. This is a writer who knows the grammars of Standard English and of Jamaican creole, who is writing in a context where Standard English is demanded, and whose unconscious use of creole forms in writing occurs where the spoken versions of the two language forms are most similar. It is clear that Pat needs to acquire more consistent use of Standard English for the particular purpose of writing she is engaged in here. Most teachers would believe this unlikely to be achieved if her own language were devalued or the options available to her were reduced by a prescription that only Standard English should be used for all purposes.

The above example has been drawn from contexts of use for British Black English and it should be noted that there are parallel situations in other cultures and that there has been, for example, extensive analysis and discussion of Black American English both in the work of American sociolinguists such as William Labov and in the language and literacy work of many American educationalists.

See also **accent, creole, dialect, Standard English**
Further reading Edwards, 1979; Labov, 1972; Richmond, 1982; Sebba, 1993; Sutcliffe, 1983; Sutcliffe and Wong (eds), 1986

British/English English and British are two adjectives widely applied in respect of institutions in Great Britain, including language. The term 'British English' is used to refer to that variety of Standard English current in the British Isles and which differentiates it from standard American English or standard Australian English. Collocations with the word language are, however, almost exclusively reserved for the word 'English'.

English is also associated with Englishness and is an instinctual ethnic identification which surfaces with especial prominence at times of national crisis. The word 'English' is used more frequently with positive, approbatory associations whereas the word 'British' can be used pejoratively as in 'British car' or 'British industry'. The adjective 'British' has the most potential for defining a multiracial, multilingual community in a positive and inclusive manner, but the associations of the language with English and of English with racial and ethnic purity are more distinct in most usage. Demands for proper English are simultaneously often demands for the proper English to identify themselves.

See also **national, purism, Standard English**
Further reading Crowley, 1989; Crowley (ed.), 1991; Doyle, 1989; Hayhoe and Parker (eds), 1994; Stubbs, 1989, 1993

C

canon   The term 'canon' is used almost exclusively for discussions of literary texts though its origins in ecclesiastical discourse – to refer to what is most revered, sacred and immutable, as in 'canon law' – carry relevant undertones into such discussions.

The existence of a canon indicates that there are certain texts which are sufficiently highly valued by succeeding generations to be considered central to a tradition of literature within a culture. For example, within a national tradition of British English literature Shakespeare continues to be regarded as a canonical writer and is indeed the writer whose work has been most regularly cited in discussions of the literature syllabus as part of the development of a National Curriculum for English in England and Wales since 1985. The prescription of a canon of writers to be studied, most particularly in educational institutions, has parallels with the prescription of standardised correct forms of language. It is believed to testify to the existence of timeless, transcendental values which reinforce the notion of a permanent body of knowledge and immutable cultural norms.

The existence of a canon leads to the institutionalisation of texts. Certain texts are 'set' for study by examination boards, syllabus designers and teachers teaching particular courses; in turn these books are then categorised by publishing houses as canonical or 'classic' texts and the whole process even serves to define what is considered to be literature. There is a certain degree of truth, therefore, in the statement of the French literary theorist Roland Barthes that 'literature is what gets taught'.

The notion of a canon as a fixed set of great texts has been contested, particularly since the mid-1960s, mainly as a result of refinements in literary and cultural theory. For example the dominance of the canon by male writers and by a version of English writing confined to native British writers has been questioned for its partiality and may in turn be not unconnected with the powerful positions held by white Anglo-Saxon males in educational establishments, on examination boards and in the control of national curricula. Such circularity cannot help but influence how interpretations of the constitution of a national literary heritage are shaped. It is also necessary to recognise that canons are not immutable. The recent admission to the canon of English literature of the writer John Clare and the corresponding relative relegation of eighteenth-century writers such as Gray and Collins indicate how tastes change and evaluations shift as a part of a process of canon formation, with which definitions of what literature is and what it is for are inextricably bound.

Canons are being simultaneously questioned and negotiated, asserted and imposed, relativised and dismissed. The notion of a canon of great literary texts will be at its most problematised at times when national curricula are being evolved and definitions of what constitutes a national heritage are inevitably foregrounded.

See also **culture, literature, national, Shakespeare**
Further reading Birch, 1989

cohesion Two major means can be identified by which a series of sentences or utterances cohere to create a meaningful text. 'Coherence' refers to the underlying semantic unity by which the reader or listener perceives that propositions, actions or events fit together. 'Cohesion' refers to the grammatical means by which the elements are linked, usually at sentence level. The most common forms of grammatical connection are:

1 *reference*, by the use of:
   - personal pronouns, such as *she, he, they, it* referring to a preceding full lexical noun. (e.g. The woman crossed the road. She was wearing a blue scarf.)
   - the definite article, *the* (e.g. It was raining. The rain was cold.)
   - deictics, such as *this, that, these, those*. (e.g. There are two sets of books. I'll take these.)
   - comparative forms, such as *other*. (e.g. There were two men. One was young. The other was middle-aged.)
2 *substitution*,
   by the use of pro-forms, such as *do, so, one(s)*, which stand in for full lexical words or phrases (e.g. Most children like chocolate. Some adults do too.)
3 *linking words*,
   of which conjunctions are the most immediately recognisable. The three main types are:
   - temporal: *then, previously, later*
   - additive: *moreover, And* (in initial position)
   - showing or result: *but, however*
   A lexical chain, that is, a sequence of identical or closely related words, can also create a strong sense of cohesion provided that there is also a semantic unity underlying the text.

It can be argued that an English curriculum which concentrates heavily on the grammar of sentences will not necessarily deliver a competence in the skilled use of English in the construction of texts. It is perfectly possible to write or speak sentences that are grammatically correct but lack the kinds of cohesive ties and links between and across the sentences that make for an effective and coherent text. Explicit attention to the cohesive properties of language is necessary as

19

a key component in language development. It is important that the notion of grammar and of what is grammatical extends beyond the level of a single sentence and that the idea is challenged that grammar can only be taught in isolated decontextualised and unrelated sentences.

See also **grammar, text**
Further reading Harris, 1993; Harris and Wilkinson, 1986; Littlefair, 1992; Perera, 1984

complaint tradition

Teachers urged to be 'moral agents'

Teachers are to be told to act as 'moral agents', setting examples in dress, language and the effort they put into their work, in new proposals promoting school values. They must reflect policies on 'right' and 'wrong' by their individual behaviour . . .

David Pascall, the [National Curriculum Council] Chairman, has signalled that he not only expects teachers to correct children who fail to use Standard English in any lesson or in the playground, but also that they should use Standard English when talking to each other in children's hearing . . .

(*The Guardian*, 1 April 1993)

There is a long-standing body of writing in English in which complaints are voiced about declining standards in the use of English. The writers involved consider themselves to be guardians of correctness and inveigh against what are regarded as examples of 'bad grammar'. The word grammar is often used loosely in such cases and is used to encompass pronunciation 'errors' and lexical confusions as well as particular points of grammar. Most writers in the complaint tradition fail to explain why certain forms are correct and others incorrect, believing in a transcendent timeless norm of correct English and almost exclusively confusing spoken and written models of language by assuming that the model for spoken language lies in the written channel. Users of the language who fail to conform to standardised, legitimised norms are judged to be lacking in intelligence or in other words, to be 'illiterate'. There are also frequent correspondences drawn in the complaint tradition between declining standards of literacy and declining standards of social behaviour and morality.

One brief illustration of this tradition is the way in which complaints are made about the use in English of a split infinitive. A split infinitive occurs when the basic infinitive form of the verb, for example 'to run', is split by another word such as an adverb as in the phrase 'to quickly run'. The 'correct' versions of such phrases are, it is said, either 'quickly to run' or 'to run quickly'. The basis of such judgemental complaints is the grammar of Latin, which for many writers and grammarians from the seventeenth century onwards set a standard for quality in language to which it was felt English should aspire. In Latin, infinitives cannot be split; accordingly, infinitives should not be split in English. A more descriptive approach to English underlines that whether infinitives are split depends not so much on definitions of right or wrong grammar but on stylistic factors. George Bernard Shaw vigorously attacked such pedantry in a letter to *The Times* newspaper in 1907:

> There is a busybody on your staff who devotes a lot of time to chasing split infinitives. Every good literary craftsman splits his infinitives when the sense demands it. I call for the immediate dismissal of this pedant. It is of no consequence whether he decides to go quickly, quickly to go or to quickly go. The important thing is that he should go at once.

The example should not obscure, however, the fact that there are some uses, such as the 'creeping apostrophe' about which it may be more appropriate to complain since instances such as orange's; Buy three bottle's of wine, get one free;

Tickets' For Sale are not simply a matter of stylistic preference but are incorrect when they occur in public uses of language. Such examples have nothing to do with standards of Latin but observers may continue to equate their use with declining moral and behavioural standards.

See also **correct, grammar, proper, spoken and written language**
Further reading Crystal, 1985; Milroy and Milroy, 1991

context Context is a complex notion because it concerns not only features of the external, non-linguistic environment in which a text is composed and interpreted, but also the internal, linguistic environment of the text itself. The features of these two environments interplay in the production and comprehension of both spoken and written texts and are consequently important for any language learner.

The main features of the external context can be identified through asking four questions:

1 *Who are the participants (writer/speaker, reader/listener) involved in the communicative event?* Recognition of the audience is a very important factor in any interaction since it governs the nature of the text produced. If, for example, writers or speakers fail to recognise their audience, then the text they produce could be either too informal or too complex. A letter, for instance, written to the editor of a newspaper will be different from a letter written to a friend; a legal document written for lawyers differs from one addressed to the general public.
2 *Where is the communicative event taking place?* Participants need to focus on the actual location in which the text is produced and interpreted. Different settings will affect the nature of the communication. For instance, children talking to each other in a play area will converse differently from when they are in a formal classroom situation.

3 *Why is the communicative event taking place?* This question addresses the purposes of the written or spoken text: whether it aims to, for instance, inform, persuade or instruct.

4 *When is the communicative event taking place?* Writer/speakers and reader/listeners should take into account the time of both the composition and interpretation of a text.

It is difficult in the classroom to create an authentic external context. Frequently, contextual features are neither specified in tasks set nor considered in the discussion of a task. Students therefore often write for a non-specified audience and so typically focus on the teacher or examiner or else they ignore their reader altogether.

The internal environment of the text is also an established context, although not such an obvious one. All textual features, whether at word, clause, or between-sentence level, are part of an environment: any word relates to those words which surround it both in the immediate vicinity and in other parts of the text. Even whole texts are governed by their textual environment. Magazine advertisements, for example, will vary depending on the type of magazine.

Being aware of the different features of context should help language users to recognise that any alteration of contextual features, whether internal or external to the text, will affect the nature of the communication.

See also **cohesion, discourse, register**
Further reading Halliday and Hasan, 1989

correct The keywords 'correct' and 'correction' are indissolubly linked. Applied to language they presuppose a single, authoritatively prescribed version of the language with unchangeable, clearly defined rules. Thus, uses of language can be designated either right or wrong and uses corrected accordingly. The idea of correctness accords strongly with conservative ideologies, particular in contexts of language use in schools, where correction carries overtones of punishment (and consequent social and moral rehabilitation ('house of correction')). Pupils who offend against correct linguistic usage can be made, by practising the correct versions, preferably in the form of exercise drills, to conform to the established order.

However, the notion of a monolithic absolutely correct English does not accord with linguistic reality, against which variation according to context is a truer representation. A variational view of English accepts that there are grammatically both correct and incorrect structures, but that there are also numerous grammatical choices according to the context, purpose and audience for the language used. For examples, structures codified as correct in most formal written contexts are not necessarily appropriate in more informal, spoken settings. Thus, 'She's very hard working is Dawn' would not normally be written but is perfectly correct, Standard English when in spoken form. And certain forms, while prescribed as correct, are only rarely used in any context. 'It is I' is often suggested to be the exclusively correct form, whereas most educated speakers of Standard English would say 'It's me' in most situations.

The notion of 'correctness', especially in connection with correct grammar, has a passionate advocacy in many media discussions of language, as the following editorial from *The Times* illustrates:

Grammar is not a series of options. There is correct standard English and there is bad English. If children want to use slang in the street, then fine but only if they know better. If they want to improve themselves, they need to know how to speak and write properly when the occasion requires. Immigrants well understand this. Most Asian parents would be appalled if they thought their children were not being taught good English. Foreigners are eager to learn the language, and would not be pleased to be told that 'we was' and 'we were' are the same.

(*The Times*, 22 April 1992)

As is the case with many such statements, the writer of this editorial is strong on passionate advocacy but a little weaker on logic, for one cannot argue simultaneously for using language 'when the occasion requires' and for only one correct or appropriate use. Few teachers and linguists would, in fact, argue that 'we was' and 'we were' are the same but few teachers and linguists would argue that 'we was' is wrong. There are, for example, occasions on which for some speakers 'we was' is a perfectly appropriate and correct grammatical choice, marking as it does both an informality and an identity with a particular situation or with a particular community of other speakers. Similarly, there are (normally more frequent) occasions where only 'we were' should be used. Most teachers of English remain committed to the view that correct and incorrect English can only really be measured in relation to the user and to the situation of use and that effective English teaching continually reinforces this understanding of varieties of language and of the options that go with them.

See also **context, dialect, drill, grammar, non-standard (English), proper, Standard English**
Further reading Crystal, 1985; Gannon, 1985; Nash, 1986

Cox (The Cox Report) The Cox Report is more properly entitled the *Report of the English Working Party 5 to 16* (DES, 1989), and is the main publication of the committee established to advise the government on the curriculum for English in the National Curriculum for England and Wales. It was chaired by Professor Brian Cox, then Professor of English Language and Literature at the University of Manchester.

The Cox Report is recognised as a major contribution to the debate about the direction of English teaching. The committee had to tread a path between public calls for a greater emphasis on basic linguistic skills and professional support for a curriculum which sees English as an opportunity for stimulating personal imaginative development. The committee had to build on the recommendations of the Kingman Committee of Inquiry (DES, 1988) and take into account the debate on *English 5 to 16: Curriculum Matters 1* and *2*, two earlier working papers published by government schools inspectors. It is generally accepted that the Cox Committee performed an act of synthesis which succeeded in giving satisfaction to several sides in the debate while rooting discussion in the many examples of existing good practice of English teaching in British schools.

Within the English teaching profession concern has been expressed about the following main aspects:

- how pupils' achievements can be satisfactorily measured according to levels-based attainment targets, which are inappropriate to the cyclical and recursive nature of language development;
- the growth of the proposed content for the English curriculum, which is disproportionate to the proposed curricular time available;
- limited training opportunities for teachers to respond to the new demands of the English curriculum, particularly in the area of knowledge about language.

Such concerns are, however, counterbalanced by positive reactions to the following main aspects of the report:

- the increased emphasis on oracy: the recognition that the development of skills of speaking and listening are as integral to the curriculum as the more traditional skills of reading and writing;
- the clear and unambiguous statement that the presence in the classroom of bilingual pupils is a positive resource rather than a problem. Bilingual pupils are a particular advantage for the knowledge about language which they bring to a class;
- that a broad definition of English is argued for. English is defined neither narrowly as language skills nor

as an exclusive preoccupation with literary texts. The inclusion of drama, media education and information technology as entitlements of all pupils was welcomed;

- that knowledge about language should not be separately assessed but should be seen as an integral element of speaking, listening, reading and writing development;
- the extension of the literary 'canon' to include a broader range of texts, including both literatures in English and artefacts for cultural analysis;
- the measured recommendations concerning the place of Standard English in the curriculum and the contextualisation of grammar within a broader concept of language study in schools.

At the time of writing, the curriculum for English based on the recommendations of the Cox Report and currently being taught in schools in England and Wales, is being reshaped. Recommendations include: a reduced emphasis on oracy; the removal of opportunities for studies of the media and a wide range of cultural artefacts; the privileging of 'high culture', including Shakespeare and pre-nineteenth-century canonical writers; the restriction of knowledge about language to a more traditional concern with rules for grammar, spelling and literacy skills; a renewed emphasis on the centrality of acquisition of competence in Standard English.

In spite of the popularity among teachers of the existing curriculum, it is likely that many of the Cox Committee recommendations will be increasingly displaced. One result will be a more manageable, but certainly narrower, range of tests to which teachers will feel increasingly constrained to teach. In spite of the arguments for a broader, more expansive education through English, the slimmed–down, 'basic' curriculum for English is likely to form the core of teaching, not simply in Britain, but as a result of international reversions to 'basics' which can be easily tested, in many other parts of the world, too.

See also **back to basics, Kingman, knowledge about language, LINC**
Further reading Carter, 1991; Cox, 1991; Evans, 1993

creole A creole is a pidgin which has become the mother tongue of a community and which is used for many of the everyday communicative needs of speakers within that community. Pidgins are the auxiliary languages in a community; they are learned alongside the main languages and used for such purposes as trading between people who do not have a common language. A pidgin is not a native language for any speaker.

Pidgins have a limited range of functions. The sentence structure and range of vocabulary of most pidgins are also restricted. Most pidgins do not last long. They disappear when different peoples no longer have a need for them (for example, when trading contacts cease). Most pidgins are based on European languages such as English, French, Dutch and Portuguese, which reflect the colonial contexts in which they arose.

Pidgins commonly develop into creoles. This process, known as creolisation, results in an expanded vocabulary and a more complex grammar. Creoles usually coexist alongside the standard language from which they derive with speakers needing to code-switch between the two languages. Contrary to the popular stereotype, creoles are not inferior means of communication but are highly developed languages in their own right. It is also revealing that in many contexts (even in some dictionaries such as *The Shorter Oxford English Dictionary*) the term 'creole' is used with almost exclusive reference to people rather than to language.

Pidgins and creoles are of interest to teachers for two main reasons. First, teachers may find themselves teaching in communities in which code-switching between creole and standard languages is common. An understanding of the nature of creoles and of the relationship between pidgins and creoles is therefore important. Second, study of creolisation can reveal much about the development of languages from more simple to more complex forms. This can be of relevance for understanding processes of development in a second or foreign language.

See also **bidialectalism, black English**
Further reading Edwards, 1979; Romaine, 1984; Sutcliffe, 1983

critical linguistics This is a relatively new field. It starts from the premiss that systems and uses of language are not neutral. The emphasis is on using linguistic analysis to expose the ideologies which inform all spoken and written texts. There is a particular emphasis on the unmasking of ideologies in public and media discourse. For example, by comparing the following two headlines:

1 IBM closes factory. Workers protest.
2 Workers attack closure of factory.

Critical linguists would point out how, in headline 1, greater responsibility is assigned to the company. In the second headline, 'workers' are fronted to a main subject position, are engaged in a transitive act of attacking and the change of the verb 'close' into a noun, 'closure', allows all reference to the company to be removed. Thus, sentence 2 would be more likely to be found in a newspaper which espoused a conservative ideology. Sentence 1 would be more likely to be found in a newspaper espousing an anti-establishment ideology.

Critical linguists are interested in exposing the political and ideological background against which the mother tongue is taught. For example, decontextualised drills and exercises in naming the grammatical parts of speech reinforce a transmissive, teacher-centred, fact-based view of processes of teaching and learning, and thus a predominantly conservative, authority-based ideology. A more child-centred view of learning, with greater emphasis placed on processes of discovery for oneself of relevant facts, accords with a more egalitarian ideology in which teachers do not so much teach as facilitate learning. Critical linguists analyse classroom language and other relevant data in order to unpack the ideologies which inform approaches to teaching and learning. Work in critical linguistics has informed both theory and practice in the development of aspects of courses in knowledge about language and (critical) language awareness.

See also **genre, knowledge about language, language awareness**
Further reading Fairclough, 1989, 1992; Fairclough (ed.), 1993; Kress, 1989

cues The notion of grapho–phonic, syntactic and semantic cues applies to the concept of miscue analysis. This form of analysis represents a significant development in the assessment of reading in recent years. It involves children reading out a text aloud whilst an adult makes notes on a second copy of the text, paying special attention to deviations from the actual text.

'Miscue', as a term, was coined by the American linguist and reading specialist Kenneth Goodman, because it more satisfactorily represented a child's attempts to make sense of a text than the term 'mistake'. Miscue analysis, therefore, has an important diagnostic function, and cues are graded along three dimensions:

1 grapho–phonic cues   sound–symbol relationships
2 syntactic cues   grammatical expectation
3 semantic cues   expectation of meaning

Given the danger of relying on the evidence of an oral reading of an unprepared text, such cues might well, at different levels of language comprehension, give the teacher insights into:

- consistent *patterns* of miscue;
- what positive strategies for decoding a pupil is using;
- what supports are available for interpreting meaning;

- how the pupil might be helped to become a more efficient reader.

See also **emergent literacy, phonics**
Further reading Goodman, 1982

culture   Culture is best defined as a set of beliefs and values which are prevalent within a society or section of a society. In some definitions, the term 'culture' is reserved for the most prestigious achievements of a society. More generally, however, culture embraces the habits, customs, social behaviour, knowledge and assumptions associated with a group of people. The cultural forms of that group are the artefacts and texts, spoken and written, which represent the beliefs and values of a community.

Programmes of multicultural education are designed to acquaint students or pupils in school with cultures which are different from their own and which are often the cultures of other groups of people in the society in which they live. Most second or foreign language teaching involves learning something of the culture connected with the target language; indeed, in some traditions of language teaching studying the canonical literature and high cultural forms of the society's language is one of the main purposes.

The term 'acculturation' is also in use. It refers to the processes by which cultural changes occur in the beliefs and values of one group of people as a result of interaction with the beliefs and values of another group. Language is central to processes of acculturation; indeed, successful second or foreign language learning may depend on the extent to which learners identify with the culture of the target language. In a related way, some learners may not learn effectively because the teaching methods employed (e.g. the teacher as counsellor; group work) conflict with their own cultural norms (e.g. teacher as didact).

Sometimes the terms 'cultural deprivation', 'cultural deficit' or 'cultural disadvantage' are used in language education

31

to refer to the fact that some children may not have cultural experiences (such as regular contact with books, conversations with sympathetic adults) which can be of value to them in school. It is important to recognise in this context, however, that there are relatively few universal cultural values and that no one set of cultural practices is inherently superior. Accordingly, it is important to ensure that language curricula and, especially, language tests are 'culture-free' in so far as they do not disadvantage any particular cultural groups.

The term 'cultural politics' is also especially widespread at the present time, illustrating that political and ideological dimensions to cultural practices and to the study of cultural artefacts in educational contexts cannot be put into the background of discussion.

Key issues in culture and politics are based on definitions of 'high' and 'low' culture and on attendant definitions of the relationship between culture and the people represented by or attached to that culture. In discussions of English teaching the division into 'high' and 'low' cultures has particular curricular manifestations. On the one hand, 'high' cultural studies embrace the study of 'great' canonical writers, writers who are unquestionably part of a national literary heritage because their works are believed to encode timeless, historically transcendent values; on the other hand, 'low' cultural studies embrace the study of a much wider range of cultural artefacts, usually those with more appeal to a wider community, such as film, television, television soap opera, popular fiction, advertisements and popular songs. Such artefacts are studied in order better to understand the nature of their appeal, the extent to which they conform to and depart from conventional, popularised formulae and the ways in which they contrast with artefacts institutionalised as 'high culture'. Such study is widely termed 'cultural analysis', especially in the context of English in the National Curriculum in England and Wales. The connection of 'high' culture with narrow, potentially elitist conceptions of value as well as the exclusive nature of syllabuses and curricula built on these definitions are controversial. Equally controversial and contested, however, is the greater democracy of judgement which obtains in 'low' cultural studies and in which values appear to be relativised when all texts are regarded as equally valid and valuable for the purposes they serve. However, many courses do not accept any simple division of texts into 'high' or 'low' cultural artefacts and juxtapose the study of all texts in the knowledge that much can be learned from differences and distinctions between them and from the different value systems ascribed to them. Such issues continue to be central to many debates and discussions about the formation of English as a subject.

See also **canon, discourse and literacy, ideology (and language), Shakespeare, text**
Further reading Bhaba, 1994; Cook, 1992; Easthope, 1991; Kramsch, 1993; Said, 1994

D

descriptive and prescriptive

> The principal design of a grammar of any language is to teach us to express ourselves with propriety in that language; and to enable us to judge of every phrase and form of construction whether it be right or not.
>
> Robert Louth (1762)

> Our grammarians appear to me to have acted precipitately. It must be allowed that the custom of speaking is the original and only standard of any language. In modern and living languages, it is absurd to pretend to set up the compositions of any person or persons whatsoever as the standard of writing, or their conversation as the invariable rule of speaking.
>
> Joseph Priestley (1761)

Prescriptivism is based on a view that one variety of language is inherently superior to others and that this more highly valued variety should be imposed on the whole of a particular speech community. The favoured variety is usually a version of the 'standard' written language and is promoted with reference to grammar and vocabulary and, particularly frequently, with reference to pronunciation. Those who speak or write this variety are deemed to be the 'correct' users

of the language. Prescriptivists frequently stress the importance of rules which cannot under any circumstances be
deviated from.

Descriptivism is based on a view that the assignment of
superior status to one variety of language is often arbitrary
and is more likely to be the result of historical or socio-
economic factors than of intrinsic linguistic factors.
Descriptivists attempt to describe the language as they find it,
demonstrating that all varieties of a language are valid for the
particular purposes they serve, that language use is relative to
the requirements of different social contexts and that all
languages and dialects are equally rule-governed and complex
in both their historical development and current use.

Descriptivists and prescriptivists are often presented as
being in opposition to each other, although they can be said to
have more in common than is often understood. For
example, they share interests in such matters as the intelligi-
bility of language, and in acceptability for particular social
and cultural purposes. Both also have an interest in models of
language which illustrate the relationship between language
and values, language and beliefs about social action, and
language and ideology.

Descriptivism and prescriptivism are normally associated
with different political positions: a greater liberalism on the
one hand, and a more conservative view on the other hand.
Descriptivists believe that their view of language will create a
more equal treatment of all varieties of language, thus
enabling non-standard users to maintain a positive self-image
in their language development; prescriptivists believe that
equality can only be achieved if all users have equal access to
the socially sanctioned prestige variety. Both agree that
acquisition of the standard language is necessary but argue
that different routes and procedures for its acquisition are
necessary.

See also **accent, dialect, language and empowerment,
Standard English**
Further reading Crystal, 1985

dialect This refers to a variety of the language that is identified geographically or socially by certain vocabulary or grammatical features. For example, in the West Midlands of England, *her's saft* is used (the word *saft* is a combination of 'soft' and 'daft'; and *her* is used here where other dialects would use 'she'). Spoken forms of a dialect often become associated with a distinctive pronunciation (an accent). The dialect that now predominates, especially in writing, is called 'Standard English'. There are different versions of Standard English, e.g. Standard British English and Standard American English, though grammatical and lexical differences between them are relatively minor. It is frequently asserted in press and media reports on English teaching that children who do not employ the dialect of Standard English are using ungrammatical expressions and that, accordingly, dialects should be eradicated from the classroom.

A long tradition of research into non-standard Englishes, most typically represented in the work of the American sociolinguist William Labov, confirms that all non-standard dialects have a grammar which is as rule-governed as any other dialect, standard or non-standard. 'He ain't got none' is therefore a perfectly grammatical sentence in certain dialects but is certainly ungrammatical in most uses of the Standard English dialect. Children who are native speakers of a non-standard dialect are crucially disempowered if they do not gain access to the standard dialect but they are more likely to learn it effectively if their non-standard dialect is not dismissed as incorrect or ungrammatical and if they learn how to switch between their dialects according to the situation in which the language is used.

See also **accent, descriptive and prescriptive, Standard English**
Further reading Labov, 1972; Milroy and Milroy, 1993; Sebba, 1993; Trudgill, 1975

dictionary The last decade has seen considerable advances in foreign-language lexicography, which have resulted in a renewed interest in the relevance of dictionaries to processes of language learning. Dictionaries have been improved or developed with the needs of the language learner uppermost. There has been an extensive debate about the merits of examples made up by an experienced team of lexicographers and examples selected from a computer-based corpus of naturally occurring English, such as that compiled by the COBUILD project of the University of Birmingham, UK. Proponents of made-up examples argue that such examples are more controlled and can be especially written to explain key aspects of grammatical or lexical use. Proponents of naturally occurring examples argue that such procedures result in artificial language and that a properly prepared corpus can illustrate how the language works by means of real examples. Real examples make the process of learning more natural and less contrived.

Dictionaries are also emblems of linguistic authority in a society, performing the function of demarcating between what is acceptable and what is not, between the levels of usage to which certain items are assigned (e.g. colloquial, formal, slang, poetical, etc.) and between individual words in so far as they are admitted into the dictionary or not. To this extent they may be said to provide an objective record of the language at particular historical moments and may indeed fix the language for us in that as soon as a taboo word occurs in a dictionary it is by definition automatically no longer a taboo word. However, differences between dictionaries serve to illustrate the relatively subjective assessments of the lexicographers who construct and compile them.

See also **language change, proper**
Further reading Carter, 1987

discourse This is a term used in a variety of different ways for a variety of different purposes. In this context, it seems useful to identify four main uses of the term:

1 Discourse has been defined as 'a serious talk or piece of writing which is intended to teach or explain something' (*Collins CoBuild English Language Dictionary*). In fact, in its verb form, 'to discourse', the meaning relates exclusively to speech – 'to talk in an authoritative way' – sometimes having the pejorative associations of 'at length'.

2 It is also used, in a broader semiological sense, to refer to the topics and types of language used in specific contexts ('the discourse of Thatcherism', 'the discourse of high finance').

3 Some linguists use 'discourse' in a loose way to distinguish speech from writing. 'Discourse' is used when talking about speech, whereas 'text' is used when discussing writing.

4 The term 'discourse' is used in a much more general sense to refer to any naturally occurring stretch of language, spoken or written. In some academic contexts, the term 'text' is, however, also taking on this same meaning.

Most books on language and literacy that discuss discourse take 'discourse' in its second main meaning above. The emphasis is thus on the ways in which language functions in specific social or institutional contexts and on the social and ideological relations which are constructed in and through language. Interrogating language use may therefore be a way of uncovering such relations and the ideologies which accompany them.

See also **discourse analysis, discourse and literacy**

discourse analysis Discourse analysis is a relatively new discipline, which attempts to identify and describe linguistic regularities and irregularities in utterances which cannot be accounted for at a grammatical level (i.e. they operate above sentence level).

For example, the following two texts (the first spoken, the second written) contain no grammatical irregularities, but seem distinctly odd:

1 *Teacher*: What is the capital of Outer Mongolia?
  Pupil: Yes, I'll do that for you.
2 Once upon a time there lived a small green frog called Freda. Such creatures do not normally live long in captivity.

The analysis of discourse, is, therefore, the analysis of language *in use* across sentence boundaries and aims to create descriptive frameworks which try to account for how such texts are organised.

There have been several attempts recently to describe the nature of spoken language interchange. For example, researchers at the University of Birmingham, basing their description on an analysis of teacher–pupil talk in the classroom, established the basic notion of exchange structure. A typical conversational interaction between teacher and pupil would be structured as:

1 initiation (mainly teacher-led)
2 response   (mainly pupil reply)
3 feedback   (mainly evaluation by teacher)

An example would be:

Teacher: Can you tell me why you eat all that food? (initiation)
Pupil: To keep you strong. (response)
Teacher: To keep you strong. Yes. To keep you strong. (feedback)

It is important to note that such analysis is not essentially interested in such structures from an educational viewpoint. The main aim is to provide a model of discourse which will be appropriate for all conversational interaction. It is significant that the exchange structure most often produced in the classroom seems to occur elsewhere only in a limited way, for example, in job interviews, legal exchanges and doctor–patient interviews.

In longitudinal research into Bristol children talking at home and at school, researchers have developed a description of conversational interaction between adult and pupil and teacher and pupil from similar perspectives. The main conclusions are that:

- children need to be *actively* involved in their own learning.
- it is the role of the adult to be guider, supporter and encourager.

It will be clear from these examples that results of the analysis of spoken discourse can be of value to teachers and that, in general, discourse analysis is properly concerned with the study and interpretation of the relationship between language and its contexts.

Discourse analysis of written text is also a rapidly developing field of investigation. The areas of study here are also valuable to teachers in so far as methods and results of analysis can enable them to identify strengths and weaknesses in their students' construction of long stretches of written language. For example, the following text lacks both coherence and relevant cohesive properties:

> The giant ant is very very, big. All the children run away and the dogs grumble. And we stare at t.v. all the houses fall down. Its eyes are large and beamey. Paul and I get on our bikes and ride fast, the blue and cream buses colaps with the big ant.

Analysis of this piece of written discourse reveals an inconsistent use of pronouns, an absence of a continuing chain of lexical words, a constant switching of subjects and the introduction of new information which is not adequately contextualised for the reader. Although in some respects there is an imaginative use of language, the text does not 'hang together'. It is the task of written discourse analysis to explain the principles by which texts are organised across units of language larger than a single clause or sentence.

Discourse analysis has also been applied to the study of a wide range of literary and non-literary texts, including examples of popular fiction, advertisements and newspaper headlines and reports.

See also **cohesion, context, educational linguistics, stylistics, text**
Further reading Cook, 1990, 1992; Coulthard, 1985; McCarthy, 1991; McCarthy and Carter, 1994; Nunan, 1993; Stubbs, 1983; Wells, 1987

discourse and literacy   The term 'discourse' is used in many different ways in literacy studies but one main meaning has emerged and is now widely employed. This meaning is that discourse is a particular set of beliefs, values and attitudes, which are embedded in social and cultural practices and which shape the identity of those associated with it. Discourse in this meaning is manifested in language, most saliently in the way conversations, arguments, written reports, narratives, etc. are conducted. At this level the patterns of discourse can be analysed linguistically, usually within a framework of what is now widely known as discourse analysis.

However, discourse in its main meaning goes beyond language, and involves social roles and identities, remaining always inherently ideological. Discourses are often best defined in relation to other discourses, for internalising and becoming membershipped within one discourse often means dissociating oneself from others. The discourses of a society also exist not just differentially but also hierarchically. Some discourses are more highly valued than others and in turn may be those which are the most dominant discourses within a society. Access to certain discourses can be socially empowering.

In the development of literacy, learning a variety of linguistic practices, mainly involving print, and being successful in institutionally administered tests of competence in these discourses constitutes a large part of literacy education. In the early years learning to decode print is a central discourse competence; at the point of transition from school to work, say, at the age of 16, mastering the skills of essay writing, knowing how and when to use Standard English forms and demonstrating understanding of the sociolinguistic rules of formal interviews are among the main required mainstream discourses. These discourses may each conflict with other discourses that language users may possess or may prefer to identify with, but the socially dominant discourses in the practice of literacy, reinforced and valorised by schools and by examination systems, are normally those that confer access to jobs, goods, and what is judged to be educational and economic success within a social and cultural system. In this context therefore we might also speak of the discourse of formal interviews, the discourse of written argumentation or the discourse of 'speaking properly'.

See also **discourse analysis, genre, language and empowerment**
Further reading Cope and Kalantzis (eds) 1993; Gee, 1990; Griffiths, 1992; Kress, 1993; Street, 1984

drills The attachment to drills reveals a commitment to a transmissive pedagogy in which teachers instruct pupils in the correct forms of the language, using techniques which allow pupils regular practice in the appropriation of these forms. The word 'drill' is revealing in that it derives in an important sense from the army parade ground. It encodes an armed-services view of the individual learner who is required to march in step with a series of commands or, at least, instructions issued by someone invested with an unambiguous authority. If at first the individual cannot appropriate the required linguistic behaviour, then this can be corrected by further instruction and practice. In fact, the learner is not seen as an

43

autonomous individual learner but only as a member of an amorphous but significantly uniform body who performs actions in the same way as others. Drills thus ensure uniform linguistic behaviour according to the rules and regulations of an established authority to which individual differences are required to be submitted. Marching in uniform and standardised linguistic steps with others ensures a language without differences, distinctions or variations. Language drills provide the all-important framework of order within which differences are eradicated and homogeneity promoted. The advocacy of grammar drills and of regular phonics-based drills in the teaching of reading has been a pervasive feature of current literacy debates in Britain during the late 1980s and early 1990s with the right wing commanding both power and the related political initiatives conferred by the power. In their opposition to drills, teachers' support for more individualised, personalised and discovery-based approaches to learning and for a pedagogic sensitivity to a continuum of linguistic repertoires (from dialectal to standard versions of English) is branded as 'liberal' and blamed for what are asserted to be declining levels of literacy.

The following extract from a book of English practice exercises illustrates a drills-based approach to English language development:

81–88   Turn these nouns into adjectives by adding a suffix. Put them in columns of those that end in **ish** and that end in **ful**.

Sheep   beauty   hope   fever   grace   fool

child   cheer

ish	ful
....	....
....	....
....	....
....	....

Underline the correct alternative to complete the sentences.

89 Haven't you (any/no) shoes my size?
90 There are (any/no) shoes your size.
91 There is (anything/nothing) left.
92 We haven't (anything/nothing) left.
93 There were (any/none) of the books I wanted.
94 They didn't have (any/none) of the books I wanted.
95 Isn't there (anyone/no one) here to help?
96 There is (anyone/no one) here to help.

97–100 Can you put these words into alphabetical order?

mantelpiece   manage   manager   Managua

(1) ....
(2) ....
(3) ....
(4) ....

The examples here take a static view of language. The emphasis is on choosing correct words within a phrase or sentence. The uses of the language are internal to the system of the language; there is accordingly no emphasis on its use in a context. There is no clear purpose to the writing beyond the choice of correct words and there is no audience, other than the teacher or examiner to take account of. There are no dynamic, interactive dimensions to the language required and the examples provide little evidence of the students' ability to use vocabulary appropriately. Since the context or style of the text is not emphasised, the functions of particular features of language, the relationship *between* words and the existence of particular patterns across sentences are left out of account.

The main emphasis is thus on a static, decontextualised view of language as a particular set of forms. Above all, the assumption is that language exists wholly in a written form and not that written and spoken language coexist. For example, items 89–96 assert the need for a correct alternative. There are indeed correct alternatives for written English but

45

another alternative here is double negatives, which are common in a high proportion of non-standard Englishes and which are acceptably correct in some informal kinds of spoken English. Drills rarely allow for choice according to context, and the imposition of one alternative, applied insistently, can confuse and undermine the confidence of students. Advocates of a drills-based approach point to the advantages of an unambiguous answer, arguing that alternatives confuse and that often only one answer is realistically correct for most purposes; they also stress that exercises of this kind improve lexical fitness in a more structured and systematic way than a more 'random' exposure to words.

See also **grammar**
Further reading Carter, 1990b

educational linguistics   The term 'educational linguistics' is often employed as a parallel to applied linguistics. However, 'applied linguistics' tends to be used to describe applications of linguistics to second or foreign language learning and teaching, whereas educational linguistics is more frequently used in relation to first language learning and teaching.

The applications of linguistics to language education in general and to English teaching in particular have not always been successful. During the 1960s and 1970s applications tended to concentrate on those small units of language such as phonemes and grammatical phrases which, being the most easily controlled and formalised, had been the main focus for linguistic research. Although such insights were often valuable in studies of early language development, their relevance to the development of more advanced literacy skills, in which larger units of language and the formulation of meanings are crucial, was not always apparent.

In the 1980s developments in text linguistics, discourse analysis, and functional grammar have provided a basis for examining higher-level patterns of language across complete texts. Such descriptions of language make clear the centrality of such sociolinguistic factors as the context, purpose and audience for language use and for the making of meanings. The focus by educational linguists on the salience of such descriptions of language for children's learning has resulted in a considerable increase in interest in the relationship between linguistics and education.

The most successful educational linguistic applications remain, however, those which do not rely exclusively on the contributions of linguistics to our understanding of the nature and uses of language, but which also recognise that the insights of educationists, philosophers, sociologists, psychologists, and cultural and literary theories, also have a continuing relevance to the central role of language in education.

See also **applied linguistics**
Further reading Brumfit (ed.), 1995; Stubbs, 1986; Stubbs and Hillier (eds), 1983

emergent literacy This is a view of literacy and the teaching of literacy skills which stresses its developmental aspects. There is also a focus on what the child can do, the innate skills which every child has and has the capacity to exploit. Theories of emergent literacy underline the integrated and mutually reinforcing nature of literacy skills development. For example, the integration of early reading and writing experiences is stressed. In pedagogic practice teachers encourage the processes of learning by supporting children's hypotheses about the adult language system and by fostering their growing approximations to it. Recognising such processes of development means that children's language is not seen as 'incorrect' but rather as a series of incomplete stages through which they pass towards a more complete mastery. Teaching methods are predicated on helping children to become active learners of language, rather than passive recipients of correct forms which have to be learned.

Critics of emergent literacy argue that it is an essentially unstructured approach, excessively centred on the individual child and gives rise to pedagogic practices which are wholly inappropriate for teaching large classes.

See also **cues, literacy, personal growth, spelling**
Further reading Bissex, 1980; Evans, 1993; Garton and Pratt, 1989; Hall, 1987; Wells, 1987

empowerment see **language and empowerment**

English The definition of English is complicated by the fact that the word carries three main meanings simultaneously: it refers to a language, to a nation, and to a subject of study. 'English' is further complicated by being at the same time the instrument with which the study is done. Attempts to draw boundaries for English as a subject cannot therefore be easily disconnected from linguistic issues, from questions of a national cultural heritage and from geographical borders. Contemporary linguistic debates pay particular attention therefore to the national significance of language and to the extent to which Standard English should be a target for competence and an object of study. In the study of 'English' literature debates focus on the extent to which the national literature of the 'English' is sufficiently inclusive, and on whether 'literatures in English' are a more appropriate focus allowing as the term does for the study of writing in English by writers from other English-speaking countries or by writers for whom English is not a native language. This uncertainty is articulated in institutional definitions of departments of English as, respectively, English Language, English Linguistics, English Language and Literature, English Studies, English Literary and Cultural Studies, Communication Studies, etc. Attempts to replace English by supposedly more neutral terms such as 'communication' or 'language and communication studies' have largely failed, although the term 'cultural studies' as a framework for the study, including linguistic study, of a range of cultural artefacts is gaining ground.

For the purposes of the National Curriculum for English in Schools in England and Wales, the Cox Report (DES, 1989)

49

defined five main 'views' of English: 'cultural heritage' (the study of high culture, especially canonical English literature); 'cultural analysis' (the linguistic and social analysis of a range of cultural artefacts, ranging from popular fiction to canonical poetry to advertisements); 'cross-curricular' (learning to use language across the whole curriculum); 'adult needs' (English as a set of functional communicative skills for use in the workplace); 'personal growth' (use of literary and other texts to foster personal development and imaginative growth). These interpretations do represent an accurate collective view of the subject of English, but potential tensions and contradictions between these views are clear. For example, 'adult needs' and 'personal growth' are not easily reconcilable within most English curricula.

See also **British/English, canon, Cox (The Cox Report), culture, linguistics, literary language, literature, multilingualism, personal growth, romantics and reactionaries, Standard English, text**
Further reading Easthope, 1991; Evans, 1993; Goodson and Medway (eds), 1990; Keen, 1992

G

gender   The relationship between language and gender has been extensively studied during the last decade. The study of the ways in which gender is marked in different languages is important for purposes of language learning and contrastive study can form the basis for courses in knowledge about language or language awareness. The main emphasis and interest has, however, been on the ways in which men and women are differently positioned, usually to the disadvantage of women, by particular uses of language. The term normally used for such studies is feminist linguistics. Studies range from the generic use of 'man' (for women and men) or 'he' (*A student should submit projects by 12 December. Otherwise* he *will be penalised*), to the ways in which texts such as advertisements or popular fiction reinforce stereotypes of female behaviour (for example, that women are passive, subservient to men and exist primarily as objects for men to view). Further sociolinguistic studies explore the ways in which women code-switch differently from men, with some evidence suggesting that women move more regularly towards standard language norms of grammar and pronunciation. Some recent studies also explore differences in literacy practices between boys and girls; in them boys are shown to prefer particular types of books such as adventures, scientific and sports writing whereas girls prefer romances. In writing, girls normally demonstrate greater proficiencies in the genres of narrative whereas boys are normally more proficient in more impersonal modes such as reports.

See also **knowledge about language**
Further reading Coates, 1993; Coates and Cameron (eds), 1989; Graddol and Swan, 1989; Moss, 1989; Rockhill, 1993; Swan, 1992; Trudgill, 1984; White, 1990

genre Theories of genre and precise accounts of the characteristic linguistic formations of different genres have evolved in order to help teachers and pupils understand some of the ways in which the following two texts (written by junior school children) do different things:

> A long time ago there was a kangaroo who did not have a tail and all the animals laughed at him and that made him sad. How did he get it back? he got it back by dipping his tail into lolly-pop siarp [syrup]. The animals started to like him and then they played with him.
> Would you like it? I would not because it would be most annoing.
> The End

'Sharks'! When people think of sharks they think of harsh, savage fish that attack at sight as a matter of fact they are completely wrong. Although there has been reports of shark attacks these are very rare. Most sharks won't even come near the shore so people swimming near the shore can consider themselves almost guaranteed safe.

Sharks have special sense organs that can sense things up to 1 mile away. The shark uses fins to balance itself and it has to keep swimming or else it will sink. The shark's teeth are razor blade sharp and although you can only see two layers of teeth there are many in the jaw. Usually smaller fish follow the sharks around in hope of gathering up scraps that the shark may leave.

There are certain broad distinctions which apply to these texts. The first text could be said to be chronologically organised, whereas the latter is less concerned with a sequence of events through time and more concerned to convey a body of information. The former is chronological, the latter non-chronological.

However, more precise description reveals differences in language which enable further distinctions. The 'kangaroo' text, for example, locates events in the past tense, has connectives which order the text in an essentially temporal way, and individuates main participants by the use of indefinite nouns (specific names would be equally appropriate in such a text). By contrast, the 'shark' text, which is an extract from a longer passage, employs a simple present tense which serves to generalise actions; the text is organised not so much temporally as in terms of logical or explanatory relations which are signalled in the conjunctions (so, in hope of). The references to the shark are similarly not to an individual creature, but to a general phenomenon of the animal kingdom; hence 'the shark' and 'sharks' generalise and do not specify a singular individual entity. These linguistic differences enable us to distinguish the first text as belonging to a narrative genre and the latter as belonging to an information report genre.

Different genres are also differently staged. For example, a narrative genre may be divided into four main stages or schematic structures as follows:

1 *orientation* Who are the participants? When did the action take place? Where?
2 *complicating action* What happened then? What problems occurred?
3 *resolution* How was the problem resolved?
4 *coda* What moral can be drawn from the action?

In the 'kangaroo' text, it can be seen that the first sentence encapsulates both orientation and complicating action. The second, third, and fourth sentences involve a resolution, and the final two sentences a (personalised) coda. A report genre is more simply constructed, with a stage in which the phenomenon is generally defined, and a stage in which information about the specific characteristics of the phenomenon is given. Thus, in the following report text by a 6–year–old child, the first sentence has a structure of general classification:

> The Bat
> The bat is a nocturnal animal. It lives in the dark there are long nosed bats and mouse eared bats also lettuce winged bats Bats hunt at nittg the sleep in the day and are very shy.

Genre theory is controversial but it has been influential in teacher training courses and in the development of classroom materials. Theory and practice have been developed in the United States and in Europe, but in particular in Australia, within the context of systemic-functional linguistics. Listed here are what are felt to be some main points of conclusion from work with genre theory in contexts of classroom teaching:

Reactions to genre-based teaching

1   Many teachers have been convinced by the strength and depth of arguments for making the language structure of texts more visible, on the grounds that genuine intervention by the teacher and consequent development in pupils' language use are not possible unless the relevant patterns of language are identified. Genre theorists in Australia in particular, have expressed reservations about 'romantic' conceptions of English teaching which make language learning an invisible process and which oppose explicit attention to language, arguing that it inhibits sensitivity to language and the personal shaping of experience through language.

2   It has been accepted that a primary concern with personal shaping of experience can result in classrooms in which there is an over-concentration on narrative to the exclusion of other genres.

3   Work on genre theory has encouraged a more inclusive

view of authorship, especially in the writing classroom. Gilbert (1990: 70) wrote in a recent article that:

> Authorship is but one of the newest of a long line of discursive devices which serve to entrench personalist, individualist, speech-oriented theories of writing in schools.

Although such a position obscures important developmental connections between speech and writing, taking a broader view of authorship establishes a basis for more impersonal writing modes, and thus a wider range of generic types of writing.

4 A major concern is that genre-based writing practices can be inherently conservative and are designed to produce unreflective writers who will be able to do no more than sustain the genres of writing required by a market economy for a conservative society. The concern of genre theorists for a wider range of writing types, which are in turn closer to the requirements of the world of work is therefore sometimes interpreted as a narrow vocationalism. What has helped to change this perception is the notion of *critical literacy*. Here, a functional and more vocational literacy is augmented by a critical literacy designed to enable learners not only to comprehend and produce society's discourses, but also to criticise and redirect them if necessary. Inevitably, such practices link closely with the above arguments for making linguistic structure more visible. They clearly serve to differentiate such work from those ideologically conservative approaches to writing which would simply leave society's discourses intact, in so far as they were penetrated at all. As Halliday has put it:

> To be literate is not only to participate in the discourse of an information society; it is also to resist it . . . it is rather perverse to think you can engage in discursive contest without engaging in the language of the discourse.
>
> (Halliday, 1990)

Such work underlines that genre-based teaching is both revolutionary and reactionary. Most teachers are more prepared to embrace genre theory if it includes more elements of critical linguistic awareness.

5 Teachers have become increasingly impressed by the precise analytical work which has enabled central, prototypical features of particular genres to be identified. It is the same explicitness of analysis which has helped both pupils and teachers to develop a critical linguistic literacy. Teachers have also valued the overt, explicit and retrievable arguments for genre theory, particularly those advanced by Martin (1989). Martin's taking of such strong, clear argumentative lines enables others to argue with or argue against in a systematic way.

Problems and issues

Work on LINC and other projects has enabled teachers to identify what seem to them to be some problems with current work in genre theory, and which may suggest directions for future research and development.

1 Existing descriptions of genre within a 'systemic functional' tradition may have tended to neglect work in other traditions of linguistic description. For obvious reasons there has been a concentration on schematic and generic structure in the lexico-grammar of texts. There is now a large body of work within the traditions of text linguistics and written discourse analysis on lexical patterning, cohesion, coherence and textual macrostructure, which has not so far been extensively applied.

2 Teachers regularly identify texts which do not conform to any single generic structure. They are the result of mixed genres. Examples of mixed genres are arguments which make use of narrative structures, narratives which have reporting or exposition structures embedded within them, and reports which are simultaneously impersonal and personal in form; that is, they are reports which also contain personal accounts

of events and specific, person-based recommendations. It is thus emphasised that genres are not autonomous systems, and that accounts of genre and genre teaching may be limited in their considerable potential if they become too simplistic or narrowly one-dimensional. In a recent paper, Threadgold (1989: 122) puts it as follows:

> Texts are not necessarily formed or produced on the basis of single generic patterns. They may also be multi-generic. These are not random differences. They are historically, socially and functionally constrained: and we will need to be able to teach the differences between and the motivations for multi-generic and single generic texts.

However, the fact that genres are mixed must mean that generic structures exist to be mixed in the first place.

3 Work within the framework of both Australian and British genre theory on the genre of narrative tends to be a little too simplistic overall. It fails adequately to recognise that Labov's model for narrative description (Labov, 1972) is a spoken model based on spoken data. Because spoken narratives unfold sequentially in time, they do not normally have the characteristic embeddings, shifts in points of view, and complexities of narratorial presentation which characterise most written narratives.

4 Once the structure of a particular genre has been identified there is a tendency to teach that structure to pupils directly and in a pedagogically transmissive manner. Holding up certain genres as models to a whole class is seen as rigid and deterministic. A common view is that there has been a tendency among some genre theorists to swing the pendulum too far in the opposite direction from 'romantic' conceptions of learning and teaching towards more 'reactionary' positions. Research in domains of both first and second language teaching shows that we do learn effectively by making things our own, and by being personally involved in the constructing of a text. It has also been demonstrated that process-based approaches to writing, with an emphasis on ownership of

the text, leads to increased motivation to use language. In a parallel way, there may be among some genre theorists a tendency to over-emphasise factual, impersonal genres at the expense of the personal. However, teachers are impressed by more recent work on modelling which operates successfully to show writing to be both process- and product-based, and that work on genre can be integrated with more holistic approaches to language learning and development.

5   The identification of genres for description and teaching tends to be internal to the school. There is little attempt to identify the genres of writing commonly required in the workplace. For example, research demonstrates that a report genre in a junior school is markedly different from a report genre in industrial or business work settings. It also under-lines that text-intrinsic accounts of genres need to take fuller cognizance of the audience, purpose and context in which particular genres operate.

6   Encouragement to pupils to reflect on language has tended to be restricted to the patterns of language in the particular genre in focus. Instead, a general classroom climate needs to be established in which talking and writing about language lead to the need to analyse language. This can be stimulated and promoted in all kinds of ways. For example, in many parts of the world there is an emphasis on knowledge about language and on language awareness, that is, general sensi-tivity to different styles and purposes of language use. These include differences between spoken and written language, explorations of the language of literature, the language of jokes, advertising, pop fiction, and political rhetorics, and investigations of the continua between different accents and dialects, including Standard English. Such explorations and encouragement to greater language awareness are a necessary habit-forming prelude to looking more closely and analytically at the linguistic patterns which make up different genres. A climate of reflection is created which leads to fuller analyses. Analysis is not always best fostered by practis-

ing analysis and reflection on language solely within the context of individual genres.

Several of these observations are hardly new, and many of them have been advanced by genre theorists themselves. However, they have grown out of specific contexts of applied linguistic work in relation to the National Curriculum for English in England and Wales. Teachers in Britain interested in writing development are beginning positively to embrace work on genre theory and on genre within a functionalist perspective in particular. The notion of genre has been explored in detail in this entry because of its central and continuing significance for language, discourse and literacy.

See also **author(ship), grammar, language and empowerment, process and product, romantics and reactionaries**
Further reading Bhatia, 1993; Carter (ed.), 1990a; Cope and Kalantzis (eds), 1993; Dixon and Stratta, 1992; Kress, 1993; Littlefair, 1992; Martin, 1989; Reid (ed.), 1987; Toolan, 1988

graded language/reading schemes Graded readers or reading scheme books are books which are specially written to enable the teaching of reading to be conducted in a carefully graded and progressive way. In particular, the language used in such books is systematically selected so that children move from simple to more complex words and phrases and are given practice in recognising the most phonetically regular patterns in the language. Such books also have the advantage that children get to know characters in familiar settings because story-lines remain constant across a sequence of books. They are of particular advantage in the teaching of second or foreign languages.

Graded or 'basal' readers are sometimes criticised for being linguistically artificial and for inhibiting the use of real language. They can also lead to a lack of confidence in reading books which are outside the scheme. Many publishers have, however, recently developed highly imaginative and intelligently graded schemes which are written in ways which combine controlled language and natural usage.

One example of some differences between abridged readers (in which the language is graded as part of a reading scheme) and an authentic, real version of the same text can be provided by these two openings from Charles Dickens's novel *Great Expectations*:

My father's family name being Pirrip, and my Christian name Philip, my infant tongue could make of both names nothing longer or more explicit than Pip. So I called myself Pip, and came to be called Pip.

I give Pirrip as my father's family name, on the authority of his tombstone and my sister – Mrs Joe Gargery, who married the blacksmith. As I never saw my father or mother, and never saw any likeness of either of them (for their days were long before the days of photographs), my first fancies regarding what they were like were unreasonably derived from their tombstones. The shape of the letters on my father's gave me an odd idea that he was square, stout, dark man, with curly black hair. From the character and turn of the inscription, 'Also Georgiana Wife of the above', I drew a childish conclusion that my mother was freckled and sickly. To five little stone lozenges, each about a foot and a half long, which were arranged in a neat row beside their grave, and were sacred to the memory of five little brothers of mine – who gave up struggling to get a living exceedingly early in that universal struggle – I am indebted for a belief I religiously entertained that they had all been born on their backs with their hands in their trousers-pockets, and had never taken them out in this state of existence.

Ours was the marsh country, down by the river, within, as the river wound, twenty miles of the sea. My first most vivid and broad impression of the identity of things, seems to me to have been gained on a memorable raw afternoon towards evening. At such a time I found out for certain, that this bleak place overgrown with nettles was the churchyard; and that Philip Pirrip, late of this parish, and also Georgiana wife of the above, were dead and buried; and that Alexander, Bartholomew, Abraham, Tobias and Roger, infant children of the aforesaid, were also dead and buried; and that the dark flat wilderness beyond the churchyard, intersected with dykes and mounds and gates, with scattered cattle feeding on it, was the marshes; and that the low leaden line beyond was the river; and that the distant savage lair from which the wind was rushing, was the sea; and that the small bundle of shivers growing afraid of it all and beginning to cry, was Pip.

'Hold your noise!' cried a terrible voice, as a man started up from among the graves at the side of the church porch. 'Keep still, you little devil, or I'll cut your throat!'

A fearful man, all in coarse grey, with a great iron on his leg. A man with no hat, and with broken shoes, and with an old rag tied round his head. A man who had been soaked in water, and smothered in mud, and lamed by stones, and cut by flints, and stung by nettles, and torn by briars; who limped and shivered, and glared and growled; and whose teeth chattered in his head as he seized me by the chin.

'O! Don't cut my throat, sir,' I pleaded in terror. 'Pray don't do it, sir.'

'Tell us your name!' said the man. 'Quick!'

'Pip, sir.'

'Once more,' said the man, staring at me. 'Give it mouth!'

'Pip. Pip, sir.'

'Show us where you live,' said the man. 'Pint out the place!'

I pointed to where our village lay, on the flat in-shore among the alder-trees and pollards, a mile or more from the church.

The man, after looking at me for a moment, turned me upside down and emptied my pockets. There was nothing in them but a piece of bread. When the church came to itself – for he was so sudden and strong that he made it go head over heels before me, and I saw the steeple under my feet – when the church came to itself, I say, I was seated on a high tombstone, trembling, while he ate the bread ravenously.

(Charles Dickens, *Great Expectations*, Penguin, 1965)

From *Great Expectations* (abridged version):

Pip meets the convict

When Philip Pirrip was very young, he could not say his name. He called himself Pip. After that, everybody called him Pip.

His mother and father died when he was small. He lived with his sister, who was married to the village blacksmith, Joe Gargery.

The village they lived in was on the Essex marshes, about twenty miles from the sea.

One cold afternoon, Pip was playing by himself in the churchyard. He was still a small boy, and it was getting dark. The wind was howling on the marshes.

Pip looked at the tombstones of his father and mother, and his five little brothers. For the first time he understood that they were all dead. He felt frightened and lonely, and he began to cry.

'Stop that noise!' cried a loud voice. A man suddenly appeared and seized hold of him. Pip was terrified. He had never seen the man before.

The man was dressed in rough grey clothes. He had a band of iron round one ankle. His clothes were wet and muddy. A handkerchief was tied round his head. His face and hands had been scratched by thorns and stung by nettles, and he was shivering with cold.

He seized Pip by the throat.

'What is your name?' he growled.

'Pip, sir,' said Pip, terrified.

'Where do you live?' said the man.

Pip pointed to the village, which was a mile away. The man turned Pip upside-down and emptied his pockets. He

found a piece of bread. He lifted Pip up on to a tombstone
and began to eat the bread hungrily.

(Oxford English Readers Series)

One striking feature is that the abridged version changes
the narrative point of view. Instead of hearing directly from
Pip, things are narrated for us in the third person; correspondingly, a certain sense of intimacy, sharing Pip's feelings and
his dramatic re-enactment of events, is sacrificed. The
assumption appears to be that a third person account is 'easier'
than one in the first person – an assumption which is at the
least questionable.

Another immediately striking feature is the reduction of all
dialogue to the same narrative style. The abridged version
removes, sanitises even, contrasts in speech style as well as
marked dialect features. The assumption that this makes for
easier understanding may also be challenged. The effect of
both these changes is to take the abridged text farther away
from the rhythms and immediacies of spoken discourse.

Shorter sentences are normally assumed to be easier to
process than longer sentences. However, this begs the question of whether an endless repetition of structurally similar
patterns doesn't reduce motivation to read on by rendering
everything predictable and the same. It also presupposes that
understanding ensues from a simple decoding of the word
shapes on the page. The supposedly more 'difficult' writing of
Dickens is, for example, rich in rhythms and images. This
may foster an engagement with the narrative from which
understanding of the unfolding meanings of the whole text
may flow. Compare, for example, the respective movements
of the following sentences.

Ours was the marsh country, down by the river, within, as
the river wound, twenty miles from the sea.

The village they lived in was on the Essex marshes, about
twenty miles from the sea.

The sentences contrast in what they evoke. The interrupted
winding movement of the first sentence is mimetic of the

63

river's course. The absence of specification ('marsh country' rather than 'Essex marshes') adds a sense of mystery; the sentence-fronted emphasis on 'ours' reinforces the sense of personal involvement and identity with the place which is not unconnected with Pip's own attempts to establish 'the identity of things', that is, who he is and where he has come from. This search for self is also reflected in the play with names, both his own and those of this family. Such effects are not likely to be communicated to a reader by bland seamless sentences such as the opening three sentences or fifth paragraph of the abridged version.

Clearly, many problems are raised in simplifying texts.

See also   **phonics, real books**
Further reading   Luke, 1988; Meek, 1988

grammar   In most traditions of linguistic description, grammar is seen as one of the three components of language structure; the other two are phonology and semantics. Grammar is also usually limited to the analysis of structures at and below sentence level. In recent years, however, with an increasing interest in text and discourse, the boundaries of the study of grammar have been extended. This area of study is usually called 'text grammar'.

One ambiguity of the word comes from its popular use in a prescriptive sense ('bad grammar' as opposed to 'good grammar') to indicate features of language use that are regarded as 'mistakes', for instance, dialect uses such as 'I been' or 'it were'. In this sense, the word is also used, unhelpfully, to refer to all manner of inaccuracies including punctuation and spelling mistakes and what is judged to be wrong pronunciation.

In modern linguistics, there are different approaches to the description of grammar. These differences are not wilful but arise from the different interests of linguists in developing their descriptions. Here are brief notes on the four main traditions.

1 descriptive grammar

The purpose of descriptive grammar is to set out in a systematic and principled way the rules that appear to govern how a particular language is used. Thus, descriptive grammars deal with individual languages, e.g. English, Chinese or Finnish. They do not deal with universals of language. The rules identified are normally based on a corpus of data (a wide-ranging sample of spoken and written language) and they are descriptive as opposed to prescriptive. *A Comprehensive Grammar of the English Language*, Quirk *et al.* (1985) is currently the most authoritative descriptive grammar of English.

2 systemic–functional grammar

This tradition of grammar is associated with the work of Michael Halliday. Central to the analysis is the idea of choice. Each aspect of grammatical description is seen as a series of options from which the speaker or writer makes choices dependent on context, audience and purpose. The specific value of this work is that grammar is related to meaning in a way that is not achieved in other grammars, which tend to separate syntax and morphology, on the one hand, from semantics and pragmatics, on the other.

3 transformational–generative grammar (TG)

The American linguist Noam Chomsky borrowed the term 'generative' from mathematics to describe this analysis of language. He was concerned to identify a set of rules and principles of creativity by which *all* instances of language production (surface structures) could be shown to be variations (transformations) of a small, finite set of basic or deep structures. Hence, transformational-generative grammar is more concerned with language universals than with the description of usage in a particular language.

4 pedagogical grammar

The object of a pedagogical grammar is to present the grammar of a language in ways which are pedagogically appropriate to learners (usually non–native learners) of a language. Pedagogical grammars do not necessarily follow any one theory, though they are likely to be descriptive in orientation. They are designed to provide information which is relevant for teaching and learning, for materials design, and for syllabus and curriculum development. Most modern course books or grammar teaching materials use game-like activities in which structures are learned and practised through the completion of meaningful and realistic tasks rather than by means of grammar drills.

Grammar and its teaching have become central to discourses about English language teaching and learning in many parts of the world. The following examples and discussion are designed to illustrate, with particular reference to British educational discourses, the main outlines of debates. Here is part of a GCE examination paper set for 15- and 16-year-old pupils in Britain in the early 1960s. Questions of this kind about grammar constituted between 20 and 30 per cent of the total examination paper.

> Leaving childhood behind, I soon lost this desire to possess a goldfish. It is difficult to persuade oneself that a goldfish is happy and as soon as we have begun to doubt that some poor creature enjoys living with us we can take no pleasure in its company.
>
> Using a new line for each, select *one* example from the above passage of *each* of the following:

i   an infinitive used as the direct object of a verb;
ii   an infinitive used in apposition to a pronoun;
iii   a gerund;
iv   a present participle;
v   a past participle;
vi   an adjective used predicatively (i.e. as a complement);
vii   a possessive adjunctive;
viii   a demonstrative adjective;
ix   a reflexive pronoun;
x   an adverb of time;
xi   an adverb of degree;

xii a preposition;
xiii a subordinating conjunction.

The different views of language, of language teaching, and of grammar as illustrated in this representative examination paper, held in Britain by government, English teachers and by linguists, may be broadly summarised as follows:

Government views

1 The examination paper illustrates a manifest concern with measurable knowledge. A body of linguistic facts can be taught, learned by pupils and then tested. Answers are either right or wrong, the *body of knowledge* taught is definite and measurable, and teachers can even be assessed by how well they teach it.

2 The learning which ensues is disciplined and takes place within a clear framework. It contrasts vividly with the apparently vague and undirected concern with creativity and personal expression which characterises work in many English lessons at the present time.

3 Such practices will help to guarantee correct grammar and Standard English and ensure that the 'quality' of *the* major international language does not deteriorate. They will remove sloppiness and ambiguities in expression (which pupils would otherwise be unable to detect) and eradicate a climate in which errors are viewed only in relation to a process of language development and are thus not always immediately corrected by teachers.

Teachers' views

Until recently, teachers' views have been dominated by what are regularly described as romantic conceptions of English as a subject. Romanticism in English teaching involves a classroom emphasis on language use which is person-centred, which stresses the capacity of the individual for originality and creativity, and a concern that strict rules and conventions

67

may be inhibiting to pupils, and in the process, restrict their capacities for using the language. There is a particular stress on the primacy of speech, even in writing, where individuals are encouraged by the teacher to find their own personal voice. In the context of such ideologies it will be clear that many English teachers reject the view of grammar and of language study illustrated in the above examination paper. It runs very obviously counter to romantic influences on the subject. Although significant shifts in teachers' perception of the value of formal language study are apparent, strong resistance remains, on the above grounds, to the decontextualised study of language, to teaching practices and pedagogies which are necessarily transmissive and narrowly knowledge-based, and which allow little or no scope for an emergence of the pupil's own individual 'voice'and personal growth.

The views of linguists

Linguists have taken a prominent role in the shaping of the National Curriculum for English in England and Wales. Most linguists take the following main views of grammar-based teaching and testing of linguistic knowledge:

1 They point out how examination papers from the 1960s are preoccupied with written rather than spoken language.

2 They point out that the analysis is invariably decontextualised since the definitions required of pupils are *formalistic*. That is, there is no attention required to language use, to the functions of language or to the kinds of meaning produced by the particular forms which are isolated. Examinations such as those above are exercises in the naming of parts.

3 They point out that such examinations are concerned with sentences rather than texts. In fact, the text here is genuinely incidental. The focus is on a bottom-up analysis of the smallest units of language with little or no interest in eliciting from pupils how such units might combine to create larger functional meanings and effects.

Accordingly, those linguists who advised the British government did not recommend a return to the 1950s and to a teaching of grammatical forms by means of decontextualised drills. But they did not reject a formal study of language. Instead, they strongly advocated programmes of study for pupils in knowledge about language (KAL). It was felt that such a concentration was overdue, and had been neglected for too long, probably because of dominant romantic philosophies of English teaching which resisted most forms of explicit analysis. However, to be successful, it was argued, and indeed eventually accepted in parliamentary statutes, that KAL needed to be based on a wider range of analysis than grammar, and needed to be clearly rooted in theories of language variation, both spoken and written. These views (of government-appointed committees) were grudgingly accepted by the government. Governments in many different parts of the world recognise that knowledge about language, based on a variety of texts, includes discussion of language in context, and that discussion of context is often necessarily social and may be used by teachers as an opportunity to analyse social issues and the ways in which language patterns social ideologies. Such an orientation serves only to reinforce for such governments the desirability of decontextualised drills and exercises.

Grammar is also used as an emblem of what is right and wrong about English language teaching and its absence from the classroom is, in the form illustrated by the above examination paper, often cited by politicians, the media and in public debates as a main reason for declining levels of literacy. It should also be remembered that, historically, the use of drills for the teaching of grammatical structures also formed the basis for the teaching of Latin, and that the existence of grammar schools, as emblems of excellence in British education, owes much to the establishment of schools for the teaching of Latin grammar. But grammar is also employed, alongside words such as 'correct' and 'proper' and 'standard' English, as a lexical emblem for a range of socio-cultural qualities, as the following much-cited statement against the disappearance of grammar teaching from schools neatly illustrates:

> The overthrow of grammar coincided with the acceptance of the equivalent of creative writing in social behaviour. As nice points of grammar were mockingly dismissed as pedantic and irrelevant, so was punctilliousness in such matters as honesty, responsibility, property, gratitude, apology and so on.
>
> (John Rae, *Observer*, 7 February 1982)

An important issue in debates about the teaching of grammar in schools is that of the relationship between explicit study of grammar and improvements in pupils' general use of English, especially written English. Several research studies (e.g. Elley *et al.*, 1975; Harris, 1962; Macaulay, 1947) confirm that the teaching of grammar has virtually no influence on the language growth of typical secondary school students. Much depends, however, on the particular approach adopted. Explicit approaches to grammar teaching, based on analysis of individual sentences, and on the learning of formal rules and grammatical terminology, are in most cases demotivating to pupils and unlikely to result in improved language use, though there may be the benefits of an enhanced capacity for analysis and abstract thinking (see Walmsley, 1984). On the other hand, language analysis, including grammatical analysis, taught in order to talk about and construct texts for particular purposes and particular audiences, with terminology introduced as it is needed in the process of composition, may well result in improvements in writing. Longitudinal research studies could reveal very valuable results, but in the absence of systematic research studies, opinions will continue to be divided and assertions will continue to be made to substitute for evidence.

See also **author(ship), knowledge about language, personal growth, proper, romantics and reactionaries**
Further reading Bourne and Cameron, 1989; Carter, 1990b; Hudson, 1991; Woods, 1995

I

ideology (and language)   The term 'ideology' means different things to different people. Sometimes it is only used of
other people in so far as ideology is what other people have
when they insist on taking a view opposed to your own.
Thus, one's own view is sufficiently neutral or common-
sense not to qualify as ideological.

Less negatively, the 'ideology' is used to refer to a set of
beliefs, principles or values a person or a community has.
When such a body of ideas amounts to a view of society
or to the political practices of a government then it will normally be identified with a 'philosophy' such as capitalism
or Marxism or 'liberalism'. Ideologies are important because
beliefs are grounded in ideologies and beliefs result in
particular ways of behaving and therefore are involved
in the construction of social, cultural and economic worlds.
Ideologies therefore also define for us what constitutes appropriate behaviour in a society and indeed construct for us what
it means to be human. However, because they are socially and
culturally based, ideologies are not immutable but are subject
to change.

Normally, ideologies are implicit in social practices and are
regarded as the natural, conventional, common-sense way of
doing things and therefore are often not signalled as 'ideological'. Paradoxically, it is often the case that the most dominant

ideology is the least conspicuous. The aim of those with social and cultural power is to make ideology invisible, to sustain habits of language which make us subscribe unquestioningly to a particular version (or inversion) of the world.

Ideologies are inevitably realised in language use and choices of language. Thus, linguistic and linguistic discourse analysis can play a significant part in illuminating the relationship between language and ideology, in showing how ideology is connected with the distribution of power in society and in unpacking the ideological basis of many social uses of language, not least uses of language in educational contexts.

See also **critical linguistics, language and empowerment**
Further reading Carter and Nash, 1990; Fairclough, 1989; Fairclough (ed.),1993; Gee, 1990; Lee, 1992; Simpson, 1993

intonation 'Intonation' is a term used in linguistic description to refer to an aspect of phonological study called supra-segmental phonology. It refers to a study of those aspects of the sound system which operate *across* phonemic segments, i.e. patterns of pitch. This is the 'melody' or 'tone' of any utterance, usually identified on a continuum from 'high' to 'low'. Interest generally (but not exclusively) focuses on the final element of the tone movement in any one utterance, e.g.

> What's the *time*? Question (Rise)
> It's twelve *o'clock*. Statement (Fall)

Tone is therefore monitored by the degree of rise and fall in relation to the high–low scale.

Frequently, intonation patterns convey attitudes of meaning, for example, degrees of emotional involvement (the higher the rise or fall of the voice, the greater the degree of involvement):

What a long symphony!

> (high fall: indicates that it is boring)

What a magnificent symphony!

> (low fall: indicates that it is!)

Similarly, because a high rise indicates uncertainty, this pattern frequently occurs in questions:

Are you certain that it's true?   (high rise)

Generally, the tone falls at the end of an utterance if it is a statement or an assertion. In studying language varieties (e.g. dialects, registers, styles of speech, etc.) it is particularly interesting to note how intonation patterns vary according to situation:

- the variations in intonation patterns associated with dialects (e.g. Yorkshire, Cornish, etc.) and other 'Englishes' (e.g. Irish, Welsh, Australian, American);
- variations in the registers of English (e.g. football results, thought-for-the-day, weather forecast);
- intonational variation in different styles of speech (e.g. casual conversation, formal lectures);
- the congruence (or otherwise) between the grammatical form of an utterance and the speech function expressed by intonation. For example, 'She went away yesterday' has the grammatical form of a statement, subject–verb–adverb, but intonation can produce either a statement or a question;
- the difficulties of 'converting' the information flow of spoken language into written language forms, in particular, the relationship between punctuation and intonation.

An important function of intonation is that it signals grammatical structure. In this respect, it takes on the role in speech similar to that assigned to punctuation in writing. Yet the spoken situation is capable of producing many more contrasts. Consider, for example, how the following sentence has

73

to be rewritten to convey the contrasts of meaning that are produced by tone in speech:

John loves Mary   (as opposed to *Peter* loving Mary)
John *loves* Mary   (as opposed to *hating* her)
John loves *Mary*   (as opposed to *Julie*)

Traditionally, intonation has concentrated on utterance patterns and the links between them; and such patterns can be a useful focus for teachers in identifying speech/writing differences and the difficulties that pupils might have in coming to terms with the English writing system. Writing is more than 'speech written down'. Developments in communicative approaches to teaching English as a second or foreign language have seen increasing emphasis on the explicit teaching of intonation.

intonation and punctuation   Many textbooks see punctuation simply a matter of using a system correctly (e.g. 'A sentence has a capital letter at the beginning and a full stop at the end.'). Writing is simply seen as speech with certain mechanics and conventions tagged on. However, units of meaning are primarily developed in speech by means of intonation and, only to some extent does punctuation in writing reflect this (e.g. commas are sometimes used to indicate a change of intonation where, for example, one information unit finishes and another starts: 'When I've finished washing up, I shall do the ironing').

But not all punctuation choices stem from intonational cues. For example, the choice of a semi-colon is usually a grammatical or textual choice. And larger units (such as paragraphs) only exist in writing; their essential characteristics have to be learned. There are thus two basic principles to choose from: punctuation according to grammar and punctuation according to phonology. When clauses match up with tone groups, as in the above example, there are no problems. But where they differ, writers move between the two according to their expressive purpose. The following sentences show different possibilities: (1) is mainly grammatical punctuation; (2) is mainly phonological punctuation:

(1) For David, the decision came too late and, as the guard approached, he put his hands in the air.

(2) For David the decision came too late, and as the guard approached he put his hands in the air.

As applied linguistics focuses increasingly on distinctions and differences between speech and writing, so will there be an increasing number of descriptions and insights relevant to the study and teaching of punctuation. What remains, however, is the fact that there are punctuation rules and that these can be systematically described; other features of punctuation are more conventional and more closely related to the particular expressive choices a writer makes.

See also   **spoken and written language**
Further reading   Brazil, forthcoming; Nash, 1986

K

Kingman The Kingman Report or, to give it its full title, the *Report of the Committee of Inquiry into the Teaching of English Language* (under the chairmanship of Sir John Kingman) was published in March 1988 (DES, 1988). It is probably fair to say that it was and continues to be a controversial report, though much of the controversy which surrounded the appointment of the committee members conditioned the reading of the report. In particular, members of the English teaching profession in Britain had objected to the exclusion from the Kingman committee of representatives who had made a major professional contribution to the teaching of English as a mother tongue in Britain. It is indeed certainly the case that no such representatives were appointed. However, it might also be argued that the committee benefited from a fresh look at English language teaching from a much broader perspective, and that the members of the committee had a rich collective experience of English in relation to industry and commerce, schools and teacher training, literature and the arts, and the teaching of English as a second or foreign language.

The opening three paragraphs from chapter 1 of the report effectively set the scene:

1 . . . the danger confronting English today is not so much indifference as distraction.

Those words, from the *Newbolt Report* in 1921, strike a chord nearly seventy years later. The Newbolt committee was discussing the risk that much of English as a distinctive subject might be crowded out of the school curriculum by the demands of other ways of developing children's abilities, aptitudes and experience to meet the needs of adult life.

2 There is little fear today that English might vanish from the school timetable or scheme of work. But there is a widespread concern that pressures on time and energy, together with inadequacies in the professional education and training of teachers and a misunderstanding of the nature of children's learning, are causing important areas of English language teaching to be neglected, to the detriment of children's facility with words. As in 1921, indifference is not the problem: teachers are anxious to develop children's capacity to use language effectively. The distraction today is in part the belief that this capacity can and should be fostered only by exposure to varieties of English language; that conscious knowledge of the structure and working of the language is unnecessary for effective use of it; that attempting to teach such knowledge induces boredom, damages creativity and may yet be unsuccessful; and that the enterprise entails imposing an authoritarian view of a standard language which will be unacceptable to many communities in our society.

3 Our task required us to probe these assumptions. We were appointed by the Secretary of State for Education and Science at the beginning of 1987 to recommend a model of the English language as a basis for teacher training and professional discussion, and to consider how far and in what ways that model should be made explicit to pupils at various stages of education.

The committee's terms of reference were as follows:

- to recommend a model of the English language, whether spoken or written, which would serve as the basis of how teachers are trained to understand how the English language works and inform professional discussion of all aspects of English teaching;
- to recommend the principles which should guide teachers on how far and in what ways the model should be made explicit to pupils, to make them conscious of how language is used in a range of contexts;
- to recommend what, in general terms, pupils need to know about how the English language works and in consequence what they should have been taught, and be expected to understand, on this score, at ages 7, 11 and 16.

The Kingman model comprises four main parts: a part devoted to forms of language, divided up into a hierarchy of levels from morpheme to discourse; a part entitled 'Communication and comprehension' which embraces the pragmatic or discoursal components of social interaction; a part on language acquisition and development; and a part on language variation, mainly geographical and historical variation. As a model of language this is difficult to object to. There is, of course, an absence of the vital dimension of social variation, for particularly in British English, geographical variation often does not exist separately from social variation. It must also be recognised that social factors are crucial determinants on the uses of Standard English as well as on the historical process of standardisation. However, as a model of language it is clear, concise and unexceptional.

A model of the English language is not a pedagogic model for English language teaching though, and the committee recognises that there is no one model for such a purpose. It also recognises that the parts of the model may need to be reassembled as well as supplemented when there are pedagogic considerations. In this respect it is perhaps unfortunate that the part which causes most unease among English teachers – the forms of language – should be the first part.

Even though the committee was at pains to stress that no undue prioritisation was intended, criticism of the model centred on what appeared to be an avowal of greater attention to forms of the language and a return to decontextualised grammar. There is a lot of sensitivity to this issue, but the criticism ignored the many places in the Kingman Report which advise unambiguously against a return to the kind of preoccupation with grammar and linguistic form which was characteristic of English teaching prior to the 1960s.

The model of the English language recommended by the Kingman Committee will be easily recognised and its conceptual framework readily understood even by those with a fairly minimal knowledge of linguistics and of recent developments in the field within the last decade or so. A major problem in the reception of the report by the English teaching profession is that very few English teachers have attained basic expertise in this field. For many teachers of English as a mother tongue in Britain, their preparation as teachers will have involved substantial courses in English literature and professional courses which, while exploring the interface between language and learning, only draw on linguistics in the most generalised and informal of ways. For many teachers and teacher trainers applied linguistics is seen usefully to service only the most instrumentalist of conceptions of language learning of the kind normally associated (however incorrectly) with the teaching of English as a second or foreign language. The Kingman model of the English language was viewed on its publication and continues to be viewed with some suspicion and in some quarters with measured hostility.

Paradoxically, too, similar hostility to the report is expressed in the writings of right-wing educationalists who regret the failure of the Kingman Committee to endorse a return to formal grammar teaching and to give stronger emphasis to the teaching of Standard English.

See also **LINC**
Further reading Bourne and Cameron, 1989; Carter (ed.), 1990a; Rosen, 1988; Stubbs, 1993

knowledge about language (KAL)

We often draw the distinction between learning language, on the one hand, and on the other hand learning through language – that is, using language as a means of learning something else. As children learn their first language they simultaneously use that language to construe their experience and make sense of the world that is around them and inside them. Now for analytical purposes, when we want to study and understand these things, it is useful for us to distinguish between these two aspects of learning language: between learning language and using language to learn. But in doing so we also create a pseudo-problem, of how the two relate one to the other; and it may be more helpful to think of a single, multi-level construction process, in which the language, that is, the semantic system – is the representation of experience in the form of knowledge. In this perspective, language is not the means of knowing; it is the form taken by knowledge itself. Language is not how we know something else, it is what we know; knowledge is not something encoded in language – knowledge is made of language.

(Michael Halliday, 1987)

the language of education, if it is to be an invitation to reflection and culture creating . . . must express stance and counter-stance and in the process leave place for reflection, for metacognition. It is this that permits one to reach higher ground, this process of objectifying in language or image what one has thought and then turning around on it and reconsidering it.

(Jerome Bruner, 1986: 129)

KAL, or knowledge about language, is a term now much used in discussions of the teaching of English as a mother tongue. In accordance with the National Curriculum for English in England and Wales, pupils are introduced to a systematic study of the structure and functions of the English language. This commences formally at the secondary school stage and the study is normally undertaken in the context of pupils' own experiences of reading, writing and talking. The emphasis is on new exploratory and investigative approaches to language, rather than on the decontextualised teaching of parts of speech which was associated with language study in the 1950s. Among the topics for developing knowledge about language in the British National Curriculum are: differences between spoken and written English; literary language; language change; accents, dialects and standard Englishes; registers and varieties of English.

The following curricular statements are extracted from the Cox Report (DES, 1989) in order to illustrate the range of topics which the English Working Party (Cox Committee) suggested pupils should cover and on which they should be tested:

Statement of attainment in knowledge about language

6.22. In the SPEAKING AND LISTENING PROFILE COMPONENTS pupils should be able to:

LEVEL   DESCRIPTION

5 Talk about variations in vocabulary between different regional or social groups, e.g. *dialect vocabulary, specialist terms.*

6 Talk about some grammatical differences between spoken Standard English and a non-standard variety.

7 Talk about appropriateness in the use of spoken language, according to purpose, topic and audience, e.g. *differences between language appropriate to a job interview and to a discussion with peers.*

8 Talk about the contribution that facial expressions, gestures and tone of voice can make to a speaker's meaning, e.g. *in ironic and sarcastic uses of language.*

9 Talk about ways in which language varies between different types of spoken communication, e.g. *joke, anecdote, conversation, commentary, lecture.*

10 Talk about some of the factors that influence people's attitudes to the way other people speak.

6.23. In the WRITING PROFILE COMPONENT pupils should be able to:

LEVEL   DESCRIPTION

5 Talk about variations in vocabulary according to purpose, topic and audience and according to whether language is spoken or written, e.g. *slang, formal vocabulary, technical vocabulary.*

6 Demonstrate some knowledge of straightforward grammatical differences between spoken and written English.

7 Comment on examples of appropriate and inappropriate use of language in written texts, with respect to purpose, topic and audience.

8 Demonstrate some knowledge of organisational differences between spoken and written English.

9 Demonstrate some knowledge of ways in which language varies between different types of written text, e.g. *personal letter, formal letter, printed instructions, newspaper report, playscript.*

10 Demonstrate some knowledge of criteria by which different types of written language can be judged, e.g. *clarity, coherence, accuracy, appropriateness, effectiveness, vigour,* etc.

6.24. In the READING PROFILE COMPONENT pupils should be able to:

LEVEL   DESCRIPTION

5 Recognise and talk about the use of word play, e.g. *puns, unconventional spellings,* etc. and some of the effects of the writer's choice of words in imaginative uses of English.

6 Talk about examples (from their own experience or from their reading) of changes in word use and meaning over time, and about some of the reasons for these changes, e.g. *technological developments, euphemism, contact with other languages, fashion.*

7 Talk about some of the effects of sound patterning,

rhyme, alliteration, and figures of speech, e.g. *similes, metaphors, personification,* in imaginative uses of English.

8 Identify in their reading, and talk and write about some of the changes in the grammar of English over time, e.g. *in pronouns (from thou and thee to you), in verb forms, in negatives,* etc.

9 Demonstrate some understanding of the use of special lexical and grammatical effects in literary language, e.g. *the repetition of words or structures, dialect forms, archaisms, grammatical deviance,* etc.

10 Demonstrate some understanding of attitudes in society towards language change and of ideas about appropriateness and correctness in language use.

Work – in theory and in practice – in knowledge about language and, in the field of foreign language education what is also known as language awareness, is based on distinctions suggested by writers on language and education such as those cited at the beginning of this entry. Central to assumptions here is that language learning and development can be enhanced by greater awareness of and knowledge about language itself as a medium. In this respect the creation of classroom contexts in which pupils and students can view language as a phenomenon to investigate and explore is more likely to lead to such enhanced awareness. An exploratory approach is central to the National Curriculum attainment targets illustrated by the quotations from the Cox Report (above) and by statements in the argumentation of the report such as the following:

The preceding points imply certain desirable features in the programmes of study in knowledge about language. They should be based primarily on resource materials which might include samples of language data (spoken, written, literary, non-literary, standard, non-standard English and other languages) . . . and associated activities which are essentially concrete and problem-based, so that pupils can make their own enquiries, and so that the teacher can learn alongside the pupils . . . Comparative study (of different languages, dialects, styles, etc.) can make explicit what is usually taken for granted about language.

(DES, 1989: 6, 15)

In the development of pupils' knowledge about language (KAL) work on the LINC project suggests the following main points which would all benefit from further classroom evidence:

1 which kinds of language activity at primary and secondary level most effectively reveal and extend pupils' work across the whole curriculum? What kinds of *experiences* most effectively prompt pupils' reflection on language and language use?

2 What is the nature of progression in KAL? For example, should teaching about smaller units of language (e.g. vocabulary) precede teaching about larger units (structures of texts)? Should the sequence be reversed? Can smaller and larger structures of language be taught simultaneously?

3 The precise relationship between implicit and explicit knowledge about language needs to be known. Is the natural order always implicit before explicit, or can explicit teaching deepen intuitions and unconscious awareness?

4 What are the connections between KAL and pupils' developing language use? What areas of knowledge about language most effectively stimulate language use? What kinds of interventions by teachers most effectively support such development? At what points is whole class teaching about language effective and when is it least effective?

5 What kinds of KAL best support and underpin different genres of writing? What kinds of metalanguage are most appropriate for pupils at different ages?

6 What differences are there between teachers' knowledge and pupils' knowledge about language? What aspects of teachers' knowledge are best withheld, or can all kinds

of linguistic and metalinguistic knowledge contribute to pupils' language development?

7 What kinds of evidence can be obtained concerning the relationship between metalinguistic knowledge and cognitive development?

8 Should KAL or language awareness be a separate curriculum component, or should it continue, as it is presently formulated with National Curriculum frameworks, to be embedded within the main 'profile components' of reading, writing, speaking and listening?

9 What kinds of assessment are most appropriate for pupils' knowledge about language?

10 What kinds of knowledge about language most appropriately support the development of critical literacies and critical language awareness? What knowledge of specific linguistic forms should be developed? Is there a preferred order to this knowledge development?

A recent LINC-based publication entitled *Looking Into Language* (Bain *et al.* (eds), 1992), presents over thirty classroom case studies in pupils' knowledge about language and provides some basis for answers to these questions which are posed here because of the central and continuing significance of knowledge about language for language, discourse and literacy.

In 1993, the British government laid plans to replace KAL in the school curriculum and in so doing, to modify drastically the recommendations of the Cox Committee. In particular, the orientation to critical literacy and to learning more about the social construction of meaning through language is likely to be replaced by a much more traditional knowledge about language focused on parts of speech and sentence grammar and on those aspects of language such as spelling and punctuation judged necessary to basic literacy development.

See also **language awareness, LINC, projects**
Further reading Bain *et al.* (eds) 1992; Bruner, 1974; Carter (ed.), 1990a, 1994; Cox, 1991; Richmond, 1990, 1992; Wright, 1994

L

language awareness   This is a term used mainly in the teaching of English as a second or foreign language, and teaching foreign languages, to refer to the development in learners of fuller conscious awareness, often as a result of explicit teaching, of language itself as both a system (structural knowledge) and as a social and cultural phenomenon (functional knowledge). A more widely used term in current literacy debates is knowledge about language (KAL). The term 'critical language awareness' refers in particular to the development of skills of 'reading' language, for what it reveals and conceals of social, cultural and ideological practices in a wide range of spoken and written texts. 'Language awareness' is also used in educational contexts to refer to courses which develop an awareness in monolingual children of other, usually ethnic minority, languages.

See also **critical linguistics, genre, knowledge about language**
Further reading Donmall (ed.), 1985; Fairclough, 1992; Hawkins, 1987; James and Garrett (eds), 1991; Van Lier, 1995; Wright, 1994

language change   At different points in the history of a language attempts are made to fix its forms and functions in a timeless zone which makes it impervious to forces that may subject it to further change. Such processes of standardisation lead to the construction of rules, mainly rules of grammar and pronunciation, and the compilation of dictionaries which authorise which words are standard and which non-standard.

Courses in schools and colleges in language awareness and knowledge about language normally contain components of study of language change, while illustrating the social dimension to language use. Language changes over time are often the result of changes in the social and cultural formation. Conservative ideologies support the notion of a fixed, permanently prescribed or at least slowly changing version of a language; stress on the importance of language change and variation is more in keeping with socialist and liberal ideologies.

See also **descriptive and prescriptive, dictionary, knowledge about language, proper, variation (in language)**
Further reading   Aitchison, 1991; Bauer, 1994; Leith, 1983

language and empowerment   The relationship between language and power is a complex and crucial one but there has been a widespread underestimation of the significance of language in the production, maintenance and capacity for change in the social relations of power. During the decades from 1950 to 1980 the main emphasis in language studies and linguistics was on the cognitive universalist dimensions to language and, in terms of description, on lower level forms of language such as phonology and sentence grammar. During the 1980s a shift towards the social and discoursal functions of language occurred. As Fairclough (1989: 241) has put it:

nobody who has an interest in modern society, and certainly nobody who has an interest in relationships of power in modern society, can afford to ignore language. . . . Nevertheless, many people with precisely such interests have believed they could safely ignore language. This is perhaps not surprising, for the general level of attention and sensitivity to language has been woefully inadequate, and in particular the teaching of language in schools has to a remarkable extent continued to ignore its most decisive social functions. This cannot be blamed on teachers, because the same is true of most of the academic work on language which the teachers have been offered as models.

One factor in empowering language learners is therefore to treat language not simply as a neutral code to be learned and used but as a medium for the expression of social and ideological meanings. The more pupils can be encouraged, by carefully considering particular linguistic choices, to see through language to alternative ways of shaping reality the less therefore are they likely themselves to be used by language. The development in English lessons of courses in knowledge about language or in critical language awareness leads to an empowering critical literacy, a set of critical analytical skills to be set alongside skills in using the language for a wide range of purposes. This position was noted in 1990 by a group of postgraduate trainee teachers of English:

> Of all mainstream curricular subjects, perhaps only History, besides English, contains within it the instruments required for an analysis of the material, social and political preconditions of its very existence. Those instruments should not be left unused.
>
> It would be naive to assume that any of this is 'beyond' our students, that the pragmatic paradigms of 'English' which have controlled the subject hitherto are somehow simply more commensurate with adolescent abilities, that such a radical project should be reserved for (that is, abandoned to) the more analytically-inclined discursive communities of higher education. This would be a sure way to keep the majority continually dispossessed of the power which education should bring. It is one of the major scandals of traditional secondary school English that it seldom taxes students' cognitive capacities beyond recall and comprehension. As we have already suggested, there

are enormous vested interests operating to keep knowledge of our society and how it works in severely attenuated form.

(Daly *et al.*, 1989: 17)

The Cox Report (DES, 1989) affirmed that Standard English was an entitlement of all children and that it represented a vital connection with the sources of power and authority in society. Not to be given full access to Standard English is to be seriously disempowered. Both the Cox and Kingman Committees decisively rejected the view that all languages and dialects are equal in fact, though they also recognised that they often have to be treated as equal for pedagogic purposes at certain stages in language development. The Cox Committee, however, takes a step further and argues that in addition to an entitlement to Standard English pupils should also have the critical literacy which enables them to understand the different functions of Standard English in society, to appreciate its origins and its relations to non-standard forms and to be able to understand cultural attitudes to different social varieties of a language.

The position has been branded as liberal romanticism in most right- *and* left-wing discourses. For the right-wing critical literacy is seen as a distraction from the main business of acquiring a nationally uniform linguistic code. For the left-wing providing access to standard English only confirms the existing social hierarchy which valorises Standard English. In a paper published in 1989 and written as a response to the publication of the Kingman Report (DES, 1988) Bourne and Cameron address the economic metaphor employed in respect of standard English by the Kingman Committee, which writes that 'standard English is a great social bank on which we all draw and to which we all contribute'. Bourne and Cameron say,

What is not addressed is the issue of who put up the capital, who controls the means of linguistic exchange. We might well ask why it is that some people are forced to borrow at exorbitant rates of interest while their own currency lies valueless in a sock underneath the mattress.

For them discussions of the relationship between Standard English and empowerment are chimerical. Entitlements to Standard English can be justified in terms of equality of opportunity but the belief that acquisition of Standard English confers the same opportunities on everyone whether they are middle-class, working-class, black or Asian, miraculously ironing out in the process class and racial differences, is naively fallacious. For Cameron and Bourne differences are only concealed, not eradicated when everyone speaks the same 'neutral', 'democratic', 'national' language. The relationship between language and empowerment has been well put by Harold Rosen in comments on the Kingman Report:

Language is indissolubly linked to power and the irenic view (peaceful potential, as it were) suppresses the consequences. There are aspects of language which are negative, disabling and oppressive. It is not, as it appears in Kingman, a triumphant collective human achievement lubricated by innocuous rules and conventions. It operates at the heart of social conflict. The world is not a peaceful debating society. Language makes possible cheating, lying, every kind of deception, domination of one group by another, mystification of all sorts. The code of apartheid is in language, the Nurnberg laws were in language, the Bill abolishing the ILEA is in language. Behind examples of this kind stand whole discourses. To think seriously about teaching English and what we might want pupils to know about language, we need to understand the paradox that language is both potentially liberating and potentially enslaving. We don't invent language. It lies in wait for us at the moment of our birth holding out established meanings and modes of thought. To escape from reproducing them unwittingly is an arduous but always a worthwhile struggle!

(Rosen, 1988)

See also **critical linguistics, discourse and literacy, Kingman, LINC, Standard English**

language planning   The term 'language planning' is used to refer to large-scale intervention by a government or state in the organisation, maintenance and provision for learning the languages which its peoples use or are adjudged to need to use. A good example is Singapore, where the government has declared that English should be the language of government, law, general public use and the medium of instruction in the nation's schools. Additionally, and with a particular eye to harmony among an ethnically and linguistically diverse nation, it has promoted English as a lingua franca within Singapore society. The Englishes differ, of course, since the public uses are in standard varieties, whereas the interpersonal everyday uses are in more informal varieties, but the fundamental recognition is that intervening, by creating a language policy, is a necessary piece of pragmatism in the interests of the internal and external relations of the republic.

In the case of countries such as Britain it would, however, not be altogether appropriate to use the term language 'planning'. As Michael Stubbs (1993) has commented, 'Britain is often regarded as a country with profound monolingual assumptions and a widespread apathy towards learning other languages.' It is paralleled by the United States, where similar attitudes prevail:

> On the surface a great deal has changed . . . but basically ours is not a society whose peculiar genius is along the line of linguistic sophistication, sensitivity or concern . . . the exasperated know-nothingism of 'this is, after all, an English-speaking country' . . . Language Maintenance . . . is not part of public policy because it is rarely recognised as being in the public interest.
>
> (Fishman, 1981: 516, 522)

Stubbs argues further:

it is . . . a widespread and justifiable view . . . of British theory: things are done in an *ad hoc*, pragmatic, piecemeal fashion. But an absence of a policy is a policy, whether intended or not. And an indifference to languages is likely to lead to an endorsement of the status quo.

(Stubbs, 1993: 196)

The setting up of a national curriculum for England and Wales might have been expected to give rise to policies explicitly concerned with the place of languages and the study of languages in the nation's schools and colleges. However, monolingual assumptions and a view of a multilingual, multi-cultural society which is founded on the idea that minorities should be assimilated into the majority language and culture continue to prevail, even if inexplicitly and in a generally undertheorised way. The national curriculum in England and Wales makes explicit legal provision only for the maintenance of Welsh as a language and that maintenance is defined only as existing within the territorial boundaries of Wales, thus linking indissolubly a view of language with a view of nation *as territory* and in turn removing any entitlement to language provision for an individual living outside a geographically defined unit. By definition, English is the language of those living within the geographical boundaries of England; those who are British but who have a mother tongue other than English cannot therefore expect any public support for the maintenance of their languages. Punjabi is not supported because the territory of the Punjab is outside England.

Such a 'policy', in so far as it is articulated as a policy, contrasts markedly with a country such as Australia which has a national language planning commission and which adopts a view of the multilingual character of its people as a positive resource rather than as a problem to be wished away in a refusal to recognise this policy as an absence of policy. This 'absence' not only does not recognise the linguistic reality of the nation but is further deepened by a paucity of any officially available statistics, although some independent studies (LMP, 1985) do illustrate the nature and complexity of the linguistic situation for the 'other languages' of England and Wales.

Other languages are, of course, studied in Great Britain, and as enshrined in law, compulsorarily until the age of 14 in England and Wales. But choices are inevitably restricted by the extent of national resourcing. The likelihood remains that European languages, especially French, German and Spanish, will be the only available choices for the foreseeable future, the maintenance of non-European languages being regarded as no more than an individual or local community responsibility. One consequence of such a policy is publicly to foster the disappearance of the mother tongue or home languages of many members of the British nation. Equal opportunities may be addressed in British National Curriculum documents but equality of linguistic opportunity occurs only in its omission.

See also **bilingualism, multilingualism**
Further reading Alladina and Edwards (eds), 1991; Bourne, 1989; LMP, 1985; Stubbs, 1993

LINC LINC stands for Language in the National Curriculum. It was a three-year in-service teacher education programme (from April 1989 to March 1992) designed to develop courses and supporting training materials in the area of knowledge about language. The training programme relates to the National Curriculum for English in England and Wales, and almost every school in these countries has had involvement with the programme. The programme, funded by a £21 million education support grant, was a direct response to calls for extensive in-service training after the publication of the Kingman and Cox Reports (DES 1988, 1989). At the time of writing government ministers have refused to publish the training materials, but copies continue to circulate in increasing numbers and continue to be used as a basis for in-service training courses. Associated LINC material includes: five BBC Television and five BBC Radio programmes; a reader containing articles covering ground relevant to this paper (Carter (ed.), 1990a), and a collection of classroom-based approaches to knowledge about language (Bain *et al.* (eds), 1992). Carter and Nash (1990) provides further relevant theoretical background.

The LINC professional development materials were prepared in the first two years of the project (April 1989–April 1991), and were used as a basis for training of key project personnel. For the duration of the LINC programme the materials were included in in-service courses, and teachers were supported in considering the development needs of their own schools with regard to language in the National Curriculum. The primary aim of the materials was to form a basis for the immediate training requirements of the project; however, a further aim was to produce materials which would be of use to providers of both in-service and initial teacher training over a much longer period of time.

The LINC materials have the following main features:

- There are ten main units in the package; each unit is designed for approximately 1 to $1\frac{1}{2}$ days of course time or its equivalent. The units are supported by BBC Television and Radio programmes.
- Each unit is organised around a sequence of activities to support users 'doing' things with language.
- Each unit is designed to be maximally flexible and can be supplemented or extended according to need.
- Units are grouped under main headings of development in children's talk, reading and writing together with a block devoted to language and society.
- Each unit has at its centre complete texts, usually drawn from recognisable classroom contexts; the activities promote analysis of language but scrutiny of decontextualised language is normally eschewed.
- The training package draws on the many available examples of good practice in language teaching, and recognises that teachers already know a lot, particularly implicitly, about language.

Copies of the training materials are published in a printed desk-top version and are available from LINC project, Department of English Studies, University of Nottingham, Nottingham NG7 2RD, England.

Criticisms of the LINC project, which support government decisions not to allow formal publication of the training materials, refer in particular to an over-emphasis in the materials on social contexts of language use and a lack of emphasis on Standard English and on correctness in usage.

The disputes over the LINC materials and the refusal of the British government in June 1992 to allow formal publication of them has been described as a struggle between those who have the knowledge but not the power (the teachers and linguists involved in their writing) and those who have the power but not the knowledge (the government and its advisers). It is clear that the LINC materials were closely modelled on the recommendations of the Cox Report and before that the Kingman Report, both of which underlined that knowledge of how and why language varies according to social contexts and purpose should be central to teachers' and pupils' understandings of, and knowledge about, language. It is also clear that discussion of language variety entails discussion of how the nation is made up of different social and cultural groups with different attitudes and attachments to language, including Standard English. Faced with such an educational programme it is perhaps easier for a government to retreat to the circumscribed safety of decontextualised, formal study of grammatical correctness.

In spite of the ban and probably even because of the ban, the training package, LINC Materials for Professional Development, has been in considerable demand since the project ended in 1992. (The government did allow desk-top versions to be used for in-service courses, but refused permission for publication by international publishers.) Over 20,000 copies have been distributed to schools and training institutions in Great Britain; several thousand copies have also been distributed to other parts of the world and are extensively used in teacher training and in in-service language education programmes. It is ironic that the government might have exercised a more effective ban and ensured large-scale disinterest by heaping praise on the materials. A brief history of the project is given in Richmond (1992).

See also **genre, grammar, knowledge about language**
Further reading Bain *et al*. (eds), 1992; Carter (ed.), 1990a; Richmond, 1990, 1992

linguistics Linguistics is the scientific study of language; the study is sometimes referred to as linguistic science. Linguistics is scientific in so far as linguists regularly construct hypotheses about the operation of language which are then tested (confirmed or disconfirmed) and on that basis rules formulated. The nature of the rules varies according to the approach adopted; sociolinguists, for example, prefer the notion of 'variable' rules for language use, which are modified by such factors as social class, gender, social setting and so on.

Since the 1950s linguistics has been dominated by a paradigm of transformational–generative grammar in which a main aim is to draw out generalizations about the nature of language as a universal human property and in which there has been a focus on small units of language, up to but not beyond the level of the sentence, usually out of the context in which they were actually used. More recently, however, developments in text linguistics, discourse analysis and functional grammar have provided a basis for examining patterns of language across complete texts and naturally occurring instances of language in use.

This more recent, more sociolinguistic focus has more relevance to work in language in educational contexts. The study of idealised, decontextualised examples has a place in the study of language and is often a necessary first step in the formalisation of data for purposes of constructing hypotheses and describing rules; but an emphasis on social context, on functions as well as forms of language and on the discoursal properties of the language of texts reveals insights which are likely to provide a systematic support for teachers interested in their pupils' development.

See also **applied linguistics, discourse analysis, educational linguistics, grammar**
Further reading   Keen, 1992; Stubbs, 1986

literacy   There are two predominant definitions of literacy, each of which has, inevitably, an ideological basis. The first definition of literacy is the most conventional, widely accepted, popular and common-sense view of the process. This definition embraces literacy as a set of skills, consisting almost exclusively of the ability to read and write in a 'basic', mechanical sense of these words. These skills are treated as essentially autonomous, asocial and cognitive and, in many practices, are evaluated accordingly by means of decontextualised tests such as reading single words in isolation from other words or inserting single words or phrases into gaps left in sets of individual and unrelated sentences. The orientation of such skills and skills testing is essentially towards the learner as a private individual rather than to the learner as engaged, as part of literacy practices, in any interaction with other individuals.

The second main definition of literacy is more recent and represents a challenge to the orthodoxies of the first definition. It has been well described by James Gee:

> The new formulation stresses the sorts of social practices in which reading, writing and talking are embedded and out of which they develop, rather than the private, cognitive 'skills' of individuals . . . over the last decade or so, a new body of literature delineating a sociocultural approach to literacy has emerged . . . combining work in linguistics, social psychology, anthropology and education . . . The new literacy studies has its origins in the collapse of the old 'oral culture – literate culture' contrast. Out of the deconstruction of this contrast comes more contemporary

approaches, not to literacy as a singular thing, but to literacies as a plural set of social practices.

(Gee, 1990: 49)

Within the body of work associated with this second definition there is criticism of many conventional literacy tests. It is argued that the tests assess a particular narrow version of literacy which is suited to the established literacy practices of some social groups rather than others and that the tests have devastating consequences for groups whose skills are not readily measured by such means, since they then become identified as 'illiterate' and, thus, given the socially constructed meanings of the word 'literate', automatically identified as unskilled or unintelligent. It is argued, in particular, that such tests support and reward accordingly the literacy values of children from mainstream, middle-class, social environments.

One example of the (relatively advanced) literacy skills conventionally valued by most industrialised societies is what Scollon and Scollon (1981) have termed 'essay-text literacy'. Central to this ability is being linguistically explicit, even sometimes explicit to the point where one tells or writes of knowledge or information which it can be assumed is known to the interlocutor. The encoding of meaning in 'essay-text literacy' involves elegantly varied use of vocabulary and a set of syntactic devices, including associated rhetorical and cohesive devices, which explicitly signal meaning, signposting, often by strategic repetition, the 'logical' sequence and inter-relationship of ideas and prioritising internal relations between sentences over external relations with a reader. The skills also involve an ability to abstract and generalise information and experience and, in linguistic terms, are far removed from the kinds of interactive, interpersonal skills of negotiating meaning more usually associated with oral speech. Indeed, it is characteristic of literacy in such a context (a context which in many societies embraces school leaving examinations) that the oral skills most highly valued are the formal oral communications (speeches, debates, etc.) most closely connected with the written end of the oracy–literacy (speech–writing) continuum.

One major ethnographic study in this connection has been undertaken by Shirley Brice Heath and reported in several publications, including *Ways With Words* (Brice Heath, 1983). Brice Heath collected data in two small-town North Carolina working-class communities, one Roadville (predominantly white working–class), the other Trackton (predominantly black working–class), and compared her findings with data collected from mainstream middle-class, urban black and white communities. Children in both Roadville and Trackton were unsuccessful in school in spite of the fact that their communities placed a high value on school achievement.

It is impossible to summarise here a richly detailed sociolinguistic research study but one basic conclusion is that the mainstream middle-class children were better prepared for school by the literacy practices in their homes. Such practices routinely involve 'decontextualising' texts, a process in which parents read with their children by asking for the meanings of individual words in the texts, by inviting their children to talk about what they have read and by testing their knowledge of specific content. The non-mainstream children engage in different literacy practices but both sets of practices share little with those of the mainstream children. For example, for the Roadville community fictional events are not real events and therefore context questions are viewed as irrelevant; in Trackton adults rarely read to their children and bedtime stories are almost non-existent but there is extensive oral interaction, with children being encouraged to compare experiences. The focus is almost always on concrete rather than decontextualised situations.

Advocates of the second main definition of literacy as a set of socially variable practices within which particular skills are valued (and others devalued) argue for schools and teachers to try to give greater recognition to literacy as socially and culturally embedded and to the different ways with words which all children have. Children who lack the home experiences which support the literacy skills valued in schools need to receive encouragement for the skills they do possess, to have intensive practice in the skills which they need to develop and to benefit from the creation of school literacies which establish continuity with the linguistic and literacy practices of different communities.

A more plural view of literacy as a capacity to participate in certain events and to perform context-specific tasks is also manifested in terms such as 'computer-literate' and 'media-literacy'. In fact, many courses now exist which are designed to foster in pupils and students a capacity to 'read' television and news media intelligently and with critical discrimination. Though a 'secondary literacy', advocates of media literacy argue for its primacy in a world in which print is becomingly increasingly displaced.

See also **back to basics, discourse and literacy, genre, spoken and written language, testing/tests**
Further reading Barton, 1994; Baynham, 1994; Brice Heath, 1983; Freire and Macedo, 1987; Garton and Pratt, 1989; Gee, 1990; Goodman, 1982; Hamilton *et al.* (eds), 1994; Maybin (ed.), 1993; Meek and Mills (eds), 1989; Scollon and Scollon, 1981; Street, 1984; Vygotsky, 1978

literary language In one sense, literary language is the language of literature; it is found in literary texts and is, for many literary critics, an unproblematic category. Such a position cannot, however, be as unnegotiable as it seems to be, if only because the term 'literature' itself is subject to constant change. In the history of English 'literature', literature has meant different things at different times: from elevated treatment of dignified subjects (fifteenth century) to simply writing in the broadest sense of the word (e.g. diaries, travelogues, historical and biographical accounts) (eighteenth century) to the sense of creative, highly imaginative literature (with a hieratic upper-case 'L') appropriated under the influence of romantic theories of literature by Matthew Arnold and F. R. Leavis in the last one hundred years. For a fuller account of such semantic change in respect of literature, see Williams (1983) who also points out the semantic detritus of the eighteenth–century sense of the word in its use to describe the 'literature' of an academic subject, or in the collocations of insurance 'literature' or travel agents' 'literature'. Literature is subject to constant change; it is not universally the same everywhere and is eminently negotiable. Definitions of literary language have to be part of the same process.

Accordingly, most pedagogic approaches to the study and appreciation of literary language are not confined to the study of the language of canonical literary texts. One fundamental argument is that appreciation of the language of canonical texts may be best fostered by responses to those everyday users of language which are characterised by creative verbal play. The Cox Committee (DES, 1990) points out that an appreciation of the literariness inherent in jokes, advertisements, newspaper headlines, popular songs and even the names of hairdressers' shops can be a stimulus to appreciation of more complex and resonant instances. They give examples of creative language use such as:

Way Ahead
Shampers
Headlines

and point out that literary language is not a yes/no category but rather a continuum. Pupils' knowledge about language and appreciation of literature can be more mutually reinforcing if basic continua from literary to non-literary language are endorsed by teachers.

See also **canon**
Further reading Carter and Nash, 1990

literature The term literature is problematic. However, at one level it is uncontentious and refers simply to a body of written texts, produced by a culture and highly valued within that culture over a period of time as part of its literary heritage. Thus, English literature is the literature of the English and results unproblematically in courses in schools and universities in English literature with a poet and dramatist such as Shakespeare, who is considered to be the English national writer, as the core component in such courses. There is general agreement that reading such texts is an important part of literacy development and can be especially valuable in extending imaginative and intellectual development, aesthetic appreciation and an understanding of how experiences of people in the past and present can be represented.

Problems surface over a definition of those canonical texts which constitute the literary heritage; in particular, judgements over the value of contemporary texts are variable but tastes also change in relation to the texts of the past. Thus, a literary canon will be defined by what it excludes as well as what it includes. Further problems result from the extent and variation of the use of the English language in the world. English is the language of literature in many countries and not simply in countries such as Australia or Ireland where English is a first language but also in countries such as Nigeria, India, Malaysia and the Caribbean, where English is an institutionalised language of the country, although not the first language of many of the writers. Much of the most highly valued writing in English in the last thirty years has been produced in such contexts. It leads to the term 'literature in English' being preferred as a more inclusive term to the term English literature. Literature in English will not necessarily endorse standard versions of the language and may deliberately develop alternative models of creative language use. The heritage of English literature as the literature of the English is at the same time often judged to be the vehicle whereby a standard international version of the language is established in its dominant role.

Syllabuses are therefore central to the presentation of particular versions of the English language and the English literary heritage and such key words have been a central source of contestation in the formulation of a literature curriculum within the National Curriculum in England and Wales during the 1990s. Such debate has reinforced recognition that the exclusion or inclusion of a text in the curriculum is not a neutral act but reveals varying presuppositions about the quality and value of texts, about the relevance to personal experience of such texts, about the English language and about cultural and national identity.

Literature is central to literacy and the extent to which the terms are defined and redefined, often in closely interconnected ways, is illustrated by the wide range of other entries in which literature is a key word.

See also **author(ship), canon, culture, literary language, personal growth, read/reading, romantics and reactionaries, Shakespeare, text**
Further reading Cox, 1991; Evans, 1993; Goodson and Medway (eds), 1990; West, 1994

metalanguage   Metalanguage is the language used to talk about language. Without a range of linguistic terms it is difficult to conduct systematic discussions of language structure and use. Metalanguage can serve to enhance greater language awareness but knowledge of terminology is in itself no guarantee of understanding language use. Extensive research is also needed into the relationship between metalanguage, linguistic awareness and effective language use, particularly in the context of literacy development.

See also **drills, grammar, knowledge about language, language awareness**
Further reading   Bruner, 1986; Carter, 1990b

multilingualism

> In a linguistically conscious nation in the modern world we should see multilingualism as an asset, as something to be nurtured, and one of the agencies which should nurture it is the school.

> (The Bullock Report, DES, 1975)

Multilingualism refers to communities in which several languages are used and to the existence of speakers with an ability to use several languages. Multilingualism normally subsumes the term 'bilingualism' which more narrowly refers to a command of two languages although the term multilingualism frequently tends to be used in connection with societies and nations. Multilingualism is common in many parts of the world, although *one* language will normally act as a main vehicle of communication (a lingua franca) between speakers or as a standard language for use, for example, in the media, educational contexts, etc. in the community or country concerned. Multilingualism is a frequent and complex phenomenon, which has been the subject of many different sociolinguistic studies. The same studies also illustrate, however, that there are very few parts of the world in which there are totally monolingual speech communities and that multilingualism itself necessarily implies varying degrees of linguistic proficiency. One aspect of the complexity of multilingualism is that the importance of a particular language for a community or country is closely connected with the numbers and social position of its speakers and users and to an even more complex degree by definitions of nationality which obtain within and across the geographical boundaries of the country.

In some countries, multilingualism is seen a distinct problem which can only be properly resolved if there is *one* national language; in other countries, multilingualism is seen very positively as a distinctive feature of nationhood and as a valuable economic, cultural and political resource which can be mobilised for national advantage.

See also **bilingualism, language planning**
Further reading Alladina and Edwards (eds), 1991; LMP, 1985; Miller, 1983

narrative

> Narrative, like lyric or dance, is not to be regarded as an aesthetic invention by artists to control, manipulate, and order experience, but as a primary act of mind transferred to art from life . . . Inner and out story-telling plays a major role in our sleeping and waking lives. We dream in narrative, remember, anticipate, hope, despair, believe, doubt, plan, revise, criticise, construct, gossip, learn, hate and love by narrative. In order really to live, we make up stories about ourselves and others, about the personal as well as the social past and future.
>
> (Barbara Hardy, 'The narrative imagination', 1975)

Narrative is a key element in literacy development. Narratives are read and written with great frequency before, throughout and beyond school years. For many theorists and practitioners in the area of language education, narrative is a core genre, of universal provenance and often uniquely disposed to provide an imaginatively stimulating content and a natural formal shape for expression, especially self-expression, through language. Narratives are endemic to spoken language, are an essential element in conversational discourse, and are the most common written genre; accordingly, narratives can support the transitions from spoken to written language development which are essential for the acquisition of full literacy. The National Curriculum for English in England and Wales stresses the centrality of narrative for the development of reading, writing and speaking skills, though development is also predicated on the further acquisition of competence in the use of, and response to, non-narrative, non-chronological texts.

Objections have been raised to the dominance of narrative in the language curriculum. For example, some critics have argued that an over-concentration on the value of literary experiences and a shaping of the child's world through constant exposure to literary, fictional, imaginative secondary worlds have led to comparative neglect of non-narrative texts. Such a neglect, it is said, can deprive children of sufficient exposure to and practice in the kinds of factual genres, such as reports, which predominate outside schools, and which for employers, in particular, constitute primary worlds of relevance to the workplace. Others have pointed out that narrative must remain primary since other genres, for example, argument, grow organically from a base in narrative structure. In whatever way these views are reconciled in theory, pedagogy and in classroom practice, further advances depend on more extensive linguistic and structural descriptions of how narratives actually work. A number of specific examples relevant to this entry and including texts written by children can be found in the entry for **genre**.

See also **author(ship), genre, personal growth**
Further reading Andrews (ed.), 1989; Fox, 1993; Harris and Wilkinson, 1986; Martin, 1989; Toolan, 1988

national

English ought to be the queen of the curriculum for any British child. It is one of the things that define his or her nationality.

(*The Times*, 30 April 1988)

How shameful it is that so many children in so many foreign countries speak and write better English, and are more familiar with Shakespeare, than our own young generation. Now Education Secretary John Patten has ordered a back-to-basics approach to the teaching of our language. It is not before time . . .

It is time to stop talking about a return to the quality of education Britain enjoyed before the new English humbugs persuaded the education establishment that trendiness was all. It is time to get on with getting back to quality.

English is the language of Shakespeare and the Bible. It is also the first international language of science and air traffic control. It is the language that unites countries.

(*Daily Express*, 10 September 1992)

There are issues here once again concerning Standard English and our national perceptions of its functions. The equation of Standard English and Standard English as a national language forces us to consider the semantic connection between nation and curriculum which a national curriculum compels. Here the word 'national', as the dictionary tells us, means 'common to, characteristic of, belonging to, or pertaining to a nation'. Again, however, meanings cannot be so conveniently constrained. Nation is a polity, an administrative structure, controlled by legislation. Here a nation is a state with a government, a civil service and a national anthem. One would, therefore, expect a national curriculum to serve the interests of the state. Within the polity there are people. Some of them live as members of the nation but may not feel an affinity with, or allegiance to, the majority within the polity. Nationality does not of itself create nationhood. A national curriculum for a pluralistic nation demands recognition of the nation as polity and as community. Standard English is certainly an instrumental, high-prestige and necessary language of the polity, but to *insist* on its hegemony, to say that it is the exclusive language of the school, spoken and written, is to devalue the kinds of identity and integration connoted by the sense of nation as diverse culture and community. The following statement made in 1987 by a British Minister of Education illustrates how the public pronouncements of politicians often gloss over such complexities:

> I see the national curriculum as a way of increasing our social coherence . . . The cohesive role of the national curriculum will provide our society with a greater sense of identity.
>
> (*The Guardian*, 16 September 1987)

There is a kind of internal linguistic imperialism at work here which parallels the Victorian mission to export English as a language of civilisation and cultural unity to the colonies and beyond. As Edward Said has demonstrated in a ground-breaking study of 'orientalism', a view of language is never very far removed from a view of people. It is necessary to observe further that an equation of Standard English and nationalism is not new, as the following quotations from the Newbolt Report (DES, 1921), *The Teaching of English in England* illustrate. Here the main ideological impetus to a view of language is never very far away from the equation of Standard English with the national, expressed in a desire for unity between and across different social classes in the nation:

> Two causes, both accidental and conventional rather than national, at present distinguish and divide one class from another in England. The first of these is a marked difference in their modes of speech. If the teaching of the language were properly provided for, the difference between educated and uneducated speech, which at present causes so much prejudice and difficulty of intercourse on both sides, would gradually disappear.

> The English people might learn as a whole to regard their own language, first with respect, and then with a genuine feeling of pride and affection . . . Such a feeling for our own native language would be a bond of union between classes, and would beget the right kind of national pride.

110

The Elementary School might exert a more permanently humanising influence on its products if it were not for the mistake of some teachers in treating English as . . . a mere subject . . . they have to fight against the powerful influence of evil habits of speech contracted in home and street. The teachers' struggle is thus not with ignorance but with a perverted power . . . the lesson in English is not merely one occasion for the inculcation of knowledge, it is an initiation into the corporate life of man.

(DES, 1921: 21–2, 34–5, 57–60)

See also **correct, non-standard English, proper, spoken and written language, Standard English**
Further reading DES, 1921; Doyle, 1989; Evans, 1993; Said, 1976; Widdowson, 1990

non-standard (English) Non-standard English exists in relation to Standard English and can be referred to as any dialect other than the standard dialect and is therefore more accurately defined in plural (non-standard English*es*) rather than in singular terms. The use by linguists and others of the negative '*non*-standard' is not always helpful in educational and other contexts as it suggests a category which can only be negatively defined. Like the opposites correct/incorrect and proper/improper, the standard/non-standard opposition can too easily suggest that advocates of a continuum of literacy competencies from non-standard to standard and of the view that there are no absolutely correct forms of English, oppose the salience of notions of correctness and standard language in English teaching. In fact, a recognition of non-standard Englishes can easily be construed as a dismissal of standards (non-standard equals no standards). Such impropriety may be effectively countered by the substitution of alternative terms. For example, 'general English', in place of 'Standard English', could allow the emergence of a much more positive term such as 'special English' to replace the current 'non-standard' English.

See also   **dialect, proper, Standard English**
Further reading   Labov, 1972; Trudgill, 1975, 1983, 1984

oracy   'Oracy' refers to the development of skills of speaking and listening, whereas literacy refers to the development of skills of reading and writing. The parallels indicate, however, no more than a superficial resemblance for literacy skills have to be explicitly taught. The ability to read and write is usually developed under instruction, whereas children normally come to school already able to speak and listen. They benefit, of course, from the developmental support for oral skills which the school can provide, but literacy is not a set of natural language capacities. Additionally, literacy can be distinguished from oracy as a result of the high social status which is accorded to reading and writing, even though oracy has recently received a lot of attention as a result of British government requirements that pupils should be able to speak Standard English by the time they leave school.

One basic problem with the teaching and assessment of oral language proficiency is that the spoken language is radically different in form and structure from the written language. Yet Standard English is almost exclusively defined and described by reference to examples drawn from the written language. Accordingly, teaching children to speak properly can involve them in sounding like a book. Speaking clearly, precisely and with expression also involves much more than a mastery of Standard English. Indeed, as Perera (1993: 10)

113

puts it, a narrowly conceived basis for the assessment of oral proficiency can disadvantage many school children:

> Pupils who speak non-standard English do so not because they are unintelligent, or because they have not been well-taught, but because it is the variety of English used all the time by their family and friends. Any assessment of spoken English, therefore, which gives undue weight to Standard English, is measuring not the school's effectiveness, not the pupil's ability, but their social background.

Another view is that any absolute connection between Standard English and oracy is a further reinforcement of the dominance of written language within a society and culture.

Michael Halliday has summed up key attitudes to spoken language and oracy:

> In a non-literate society, spoken language performs all the functions that language is called upon to serve; and there is nothing lacking. In a literate society, the functions of language are shared out between speaking and writing; there is some overlap, but by and large they fill different roles. They are both forms of a language; it is the same linguistic system underlying both. But they exploit different features of the system, and gain their power in different ways. The idea that spoken language is formless, confined to short bursts, full of false starts, lacking in logical structure, etc. is a myth – and a pernicious one at that, since it prevents us from recognising its critical role in learning. It arises because in writing people only ever analyse the finished product, which is a highly idealised version of the writing process; whereas in speech they analyse – indeed get quite obsessed with – the bits that get crossed out, the insertions, pauses, the self-interruptions, and so on.
>
> (Halliday, 1989: 99–100)

Halliday ignores the point that interruptions, pauses and hesitations can be meaningful, but observes that oracy will remain the underprivileged skill as long as myths concerning

the forms and functions of spoken language continue to
obtain.

See also **literacy, spoken and written language, Standard English**
Further reading Bygate, 1989; Edwards and Westgate, 1987;
Halliday, 1989; Johnson, 1994; Norman (ed.), 1992; Perera,
1993; Rost, 1994

P

personal growth   The term 'personal growth' refers to an essentially child-centred view of learning in which the focus is on the unique experiences of the individual child and on how those experiences can be utilised in the process of learning. In English teaching the notion of personal growth has been influential, most markedly through the work of John Dixon. It stresses the centrality of creative imaginative growth in the individual child and develops pedagogies which support language learning through personal development. Central to personal linguistic growth are opportunities for experiencing process-based writing, talking and reading strategies. Regular contact with literature is encouraged, to stimulate the aesthetic and imaginative development without which, it is believed, rich contexts for language learning cannot be created.

See also   **genre, process and product, romantics and reactionaries**
Further reading   Bygate, 1989; Dixon, 1975; Reid (ed.), 1987

phonics   This is a term used to describe approaches to the initial or remedial teaching of reading which are based on learners being taught to recognise sound–letter combinations.

117

Phonic approaches rely on 'sounding out' words. Thus, the word 'cat' is taught as the relationship between the letters c-a-t and the sounds which the letters represent. Such an approach is also said to provide learners with a systematic strategy for decoding words and to provide a secure basis for working out the pronunciation of new words. Phonic approaches presuppose mainly teacher-centred procedures and can involve a whole class learning at the same time.

Critics of phonic approaches express the following objections to the method. First, phonetic grading of words does not necessarily result in the most important words being taught in the early stages of learning to read. Many frequent words in English do not conform to phonetic rules. Thus, 'cat' conforms to regular rules but key words such as 'there', 'their', 'they're' are phonetically identical but involve different combinations of letters. Second, in a more general perspective, about 30 per cent of words in the whole of the English language are phonetically irregular. For example, the word 'row' (as a verb) has similar vowel sounds to the words 'so', 'toe', 'although' and is in turn phonetically dissimilar from the noun 'row' (argument), which has the same spelling. Third, the books used to support phonic approaches to reading necessarily involve carefully graded vocabulary items, so that the texts appear artificial and contrived, can be very far removed from real books and may thus be demotivating to read. Fourth, phonic approaches focus on single isolated words, resulting in words being taught out of context. In real contexts of reading single words usually appear in a context so that meanings can be worked out by relying on more than phonic clues. In fact, reading requires an ability to synthesise syntactic cues (grammatical expectations) and semantic cues (expectations of meaning) – both based on the existing knowledge of fluent users of the language – in addition to phonetic cues (expectations of sound–symbol relationships).

Phonics has become a token in many right-wing discourses for a structured, disciplined, teacher-centred, whole-class-based approach to learning to read and its advocates argue that a large-scale 'return' to phonics teaching (it was used as a more exclusive method in the 1950s) could reverse what is claimed to be a decline in reading standards and general levels of literacy. Phonics clearly provides a valuable strategy for the teaching of reading, particularly in the early stages of reading development but there are limitations if it is used as the sole method. Most teachers use a mix of different methods.

See also **cues, graded language/reading schemes, reading recovery, real books**

prescriptive See **descriptive and prescriptive**

process and product These terms are mainly employed in relation to the teaching of writing; however, there is in most areas of the language curriculum a tension between views of language as process and language as product. In general, a product-oriented approach focuses on the end result of language learning: what it is that learners are expected to be able to know and do. A process-oriented approach focuses on the kinds of methodologies which promote various aspects of language competence. Thus, product-based approaches to the teaching of writing will stress the importance of learners imitating correct models and of the use of correct sentence-based grammar; process-based approaches stress the importance of learners working through several drafts and discussing changes to their text in the course of producing a final version. However, absolute distinctions between process and product are untenable, and most language classes involve an integration of process- and product-oriented procedures.

See also **genre, personal growth**
Further reading Harris, 1993; Kress, 1993; Legutke and Thomas, 1991

projects   Classroom-based language projects involve learners in studying language in an exploratory and investigative manner. The aim is to develop an approach to language which recognises its dynamic features and its variability relative to context. Topics for investigation can range from comparison of particular forms between and across different languages to more open-ended topics such as different language uses in newspapers. The data for such projects will normally be naturally occurring and collected in context by students themselves. Language projects are central to the development of language awareness and to courses in knowledge about language. Language projects are strongly advocated in the Report of the English Working Party, the Cox Report (DES, 1989) in connection with the development of positive, motivating approaches to English language study which contrast with the decontextualised, drill-based approaches to language study associated with English teaching in the 1950s. In paragraph 6.15 of the Cox Report the following position concerning language projects is argued for:

> The preceding points imply certain desirable features in the programmes of study in knowledge about language. They should be based primarily on resource materials, which might include samples of language data (spoken, written, literary, non-literary, standard, non-standard, English and other languages) and facts and figures about languages in Britain and around the world, and associated activities which are essentially concrete and problem-based, so that the pupils can make their own enquiries, and so that the teacher can learn alongside the pupils. The data are all around, once teachers and pupils know what to look for. It is therefore possible for teachers to develop their own materials. Comparative study (of different languages, dialects, styles, etc) can make explicit what is usually taken for granted about language. We all tend to think that our own language somehow embodies the 'natural' way of doing things.

Recent changes in the National Curriculum for English in

England and Wales have reduced opportunities for investigative projects, and restricted language work to more traditional domains of sentence grammar and a knowledge of more formal properties of language. The disappearance of language projects parallels a reduction in opportunity for project work in many other areas of the curriculum and a corresponding increase in formal, timed tests.

See also **knowledge about language, testing/tests**

proper   The following quotation is a composite of extracts from newspaper reports of a speech made by the British heir to the throne, Prince Charles on 28 June 1989, one week after the publication of the Cox Report:

> We've got to produce people who can write proper English. It's a fundamental problem. All the people I have in my office, they can't speak English properly, they can't write English properly. All the letters sent from my office I have to correct myself, and that is because English is taught so bloody badly. If we want people who write good English and write plays for the future, it cannot be done with the present system, and all the nonsense academics come up with. It is a fundamental problem. We must educate for character. This matters a great deal. The whole way schools are operating is not right. I do not believe English is being taught properly. You cannot educate people properly unless you do it on a basic framework and drilling system.
>
> (Cox Report published 22 June 1989;
> Prince Charles, 28 June 1989)

The key word 'proper' used by Prince Charles is seminal in current discussions of language teaching. The connection of English with 'proper' is also common, underlining how views of English and of English teaching are often encoded in terms of social propriety:

It ain't right
A new report on grammar, backed by Education Secretary Kenneth Baker, picks out some real howlers:

We was; *he ain't done it*; *she come here yesterday*; *they never saw nobody*.

According to the report, while pupils must write proper English it does not matter if they talk like that.

We could not agree less. It is absurd not to correct children who use bad English. It is a habit that could prevent them from getting good jobs.

It does not matter what your accent is – Cockney, Yorkshire, Lancashire or Scottish – as long as WHAT you say is proper English.

(*The Sun*, 23 June 1989)

There is nothing unusual about this. A recent collection entitled *Proper English?*, edited by Tony Crowley (1991) contains documents ranging from Jonathan Swift's 'A Proposal for Correcting, Improving and Ascertaining the English Tongue' (1712) – a key essay for understanding social and cultural pressures in the aftermath of the English revolution – to the work of Watts and Archbishop Trench in the 1850s reacting, through their arguments for a national language, to the social unrest caused in particular by the Chartist movement of the 1840s, to the Newbolt Report of 1921 – published after the First World War with the explicit aim of promoting English as a subject of national unity and cultural harmony – to the politically influential *English, Our English* (1987) by John Marenbon, which attacks much current theory and practice in the field of literacy. Over nearly 300 years the debates cover remarkably similar ground: the place of a standard language in relation to non-standard forms; the place of absolute rules of correctness in grammar and pronunciation; the perception of a degeneracy in standards of language use. Such perceptions are most prominent when issues of nationhood and threats to national identity and to the established social order are to the fore. Proper English is, once again, not unconnected with cultural, racial and social propriety. Nationally, in Britain at least, proper English is a social view of who the proper English are; internationally, proper English cannot be divorced from a view of cultural and political dominion.

Swift's essay is of particular interest since in it he argues for an 'ascertaining' or standardisation of the English language, which is being corrupted by the perpetual change to which it is subject. Particularly responsible for this degeneracy in language are those individuals in a period of post-Restoration moral decline such as 'university boys' and frequenters of coffee houses. In his essay Swift writes,

> My Lord, I do here, in the name of all the learned and Polite Persons of the Nation, complain to Your Lordship as First Minister, that our language is extremely imperfect; that its daily Improvements are by no means in proportion to its daily Corruptions; that the Pretenders to polish and refine it, have chiefly multiplied Abuses and Absurdities; and that in many instances it offends against every Part of Grammar.

Swift is addressing here the Earl of Oxford, the Lord Treasurer of England, underlining a connection between linguistic currency and the general social propriety and economic well-being of the nation.

See also **correct, language change, national, Standard English**
Further reading Crowley (ed.), 1991; Marenbon, 1987

punctuation See **intonation and punctuation**

purism In the famous Preface to his dictionary, published in 1755, Dr Samuel Johnson employs a phrase derived from the Elizabethan poet Edmund Spenser, 'the wells of English undefiled', to refer to the continuous purity of the language derived from Anglo-Saxon roots. Notions of purity in language are often based on national and racial grounds and are deeply ingrained in varying degrees of stereotype and prejudice. Linguistic purity and nationalism are closely connected; ethnic cleansing is a ritual killing in war but usually also involves the removal of or intention to remove, a particular linguistic community.

A standard language is usually taken as a mark of purity; correspondingly, non-standard varieties, and variations generally, including historical language change, are regarded as impurities or infections. Proponents of variation theory in language, a fundamental sociolinguistic concept, are even sometimes accused of practising 'black magic' on students; as the following quotation from George Walden MP illustrates. Walden is commenting on the LINC materials produced as part of a national curriculum in-service training package. For Walden those training to be teachers would be harmed by such impurities:

> [in] . . . teacher training institutions, where [LINC's] voodoo theories about the nature of language will appeal to the impressionable mind of the young woman with low A-levels in soft subjects who . . . is the typical student in such establishments.
>
> (*Daily Telegraph*, 3 July 1991)

See also **LINC, national, proper, variation (in language)**
Further reading Thomas, 1991

R

read/reading Learning to read is a 'basic' skill and so attracts public concern. Even in the absence of any real evidence, much is made in media reports and in statements by politicians of supposed declining standards in reading. Complaints centre on the concern of teachers to adopt more imaginative, active, and discovery-based approaches to reading which appear to reject traditional approaches based on phonics, graded reading schemes and on a 'disciplined' knowledge of individual words which can be easily measured and tested.

Most teachers accept that mechanistic word recognition is a necessary part of reading development, but adopt a more inclusive view of reading which embraces a meaning of read as 'read into', 'interpret' or 'infer'. 'To read', therefore, is a verb which means both to decode and to interpret. Teachers stress that learning to read should be more than a decontextualised skill and should become a resource which can be utilised through life, a capacity defined by Freire and Macedo (1987) as 'reading the word and reading the world'. This means that reading has to be related to purpose, and that skills of skimming and scanning texts, in addition to interpretive and critical capacities, particularly those fostered by engagement with literary texts, are essential. Early reading, in particular, can be most effectively promoted by teaching procedures which support reading texts, not simply as words

on the page, but as a range of meanings available for interpretation with reference to surrounding pictures, to the
imaginative worlds created by the text, and to the experiences
of the individual reader. The tensions between these two
opposed readings of 'read' continue to cause difficulties,
though many teachers in many schools adopt balanced, integrated approaches to the teaching of reading.

See also **'back to basics', complaint tradition, graded
language/reading schemes, literature, phonics, reading
recovery, real books**
Further reading Freire and Macedo, 1987; Meek, 1988;
Montgomery *et al.*, 1992; Smith, 1985

reading recovery   Reading Recovery is an intervention programme designed to assist early readers who are encountering
literacy problems. The programme is based on an extensive
research project begun in New Zealand in the 1970s and
nationally implemented since 1983 under the direction of
Professor Marie Clay.

A reading recovery programme is essentially a second wave
supplementary teaching programme with the particular aim
of assisting very poor or non-readers to achieve a level of
competence in reading which will enable them to work at the
average level of their classmates and to progress satisfactorily
at such a level. Reading recovery programmes operate in
many different education systems throughout the world,
including those of Australia, Canada, USA and Britain. In
Britain a £3 million investment in Reading Recovery and
associated teacher training programmes was announced in
1991 as a form of public acknowledgment that existing teaching methods were considered by ministers to be inadequate.

Reading Recovery is an individual-centred programme
which is tailored differently for each child with learning
difficulties. Each child has an intensive programme of one-to-
one instruction which supplements the regular class instruction activities. The pedagogic focus is to provide learners

with strategies which enable them to attend both to the form and meaning of the message with a constant emphasis on what the learner can already achieve. A high priority is given to children reading as many real books as possible and to assisting them with writing tasks based on their reading, so that the relationship between reading and writing is continually reinforced.

See also **graded language/reading schemes, phonics, read/reading, real books**
Further reading   Clay, 1972; Smith, 1985

real books   'Real books' is a term which describes a particular kind of book, but which has also come to be used to describe an approach to the teaching of reading. 'Real books' or 'whole books' mean that teachers teach reading using the kind of books which might be bought in a bookshop. Advocates of real books oppose graded readers or books in reading schemes on the grounds that controlled or graded language is artificial and cannot create meaningful experiences for the reader. Real books are believed to be more motivating to read, allowing readers to decode the meanings of words by using pictures, other words on the page and general contextual clues. In this respect such procedures contrast markedly with approaches to the teaching of reading such as phonics which adopt more decontextualised strategies, focusing on the correspondence between sound and symbol. It is sometimes alleged that the 'real books' approach means that children are not taught to read but are simply exposed to the books so that they learn to read only in the same way that they pick up the spoken language. There is little truth in this allegation. Most teachers use a mix of different methods for the teaching of reading; most schools teach children to read using a combination of real books and books from reading schemes.

See also **graded language/reading schemes, phonics, reading recovery**
Further reading   Meek, 1988; Meek and Mills (eds), 1989; Smith, 1982

register   'Register' is a widely used but rather imprecise term in the field of language studies. It describes variations in spoken and written language which identify the language with a particular function or purpose within a particular social context, for example, a legal register, or a register of advertisements, or a register of weather forecasting. It is difficult to specify most registers precisely because they vary according to the context and purpose of the language used and the relation the language user has with an audience. So that registers of weather forecasting can be different according to whether they are spoken or written, on television or radio, or even on local television or radio, or a national broadcast following a prime-time news broadcast.

See also   **variation (in language)**
Further reading   Carter (ed.), 1990a: Introduction; Crystal and Davy, 1969

rhetoric   The term is traditionally associated with the skills of public speaking and oratory. Many of the main rhetorical terms belong to the classical age, though they were in active use in medieval and Renaissance times. Successful public performance was seen to involve the following four main skills:

   inventio or heurisis: finding and selecting relevant subject matter
   dispositio or taxis: organisation of subject matter
   actio or hypocrisis: the performance and delivery of the speech
   memoria or mneme: verbatim retention of the speech

Studies of modern rhetoric similarly stress these skills, particularly the first three, as the broad categories within which more precise linguistic and stylistic features can be detailed.

The term 'rhetoric' has come to have pejorative connotations, however. The post-romantic era has not especially valued a crafted, structured shape to uses of language which, it is felt, should be less mechanistic and more personal and expressive. Thus, in some contexts the word rhetoric means 'empty gesturing' in both speech and writing. In the last decade or so rhetorical studies have become established within the field of stylistics, embracing the way in which particular stylistic effects are achieved in non-literary spoken and written texts. In some studies the wheel comes full circle and the language of political rhetorics is studied, in part in order to discuss the relationship between choices of language and the ideologies of the speaker or writer.

See also **author(ship), knowledge about language, language awareness**
Further reading Carter and Nash, 1990; Cockcroft and Cockcroft, 1992; Cook, 1992; Nash 1989; Tannen 1988 (esp. ch. 7, which is a study of the 'rhetoric' of civil rights speeches in the USA)

romantics and reactionaries Two main categories can be identified as far as current philosophies of English teaching are concerned: 'romantics' and 'reactionaries'. The romantic camp is in the majority. The reactionaries are probably the more vociferous, at least, in certain places such as the pages of many national newspapers, and in statements by politicians and media representatives.

The characteristics of 'reactionaries' may be summarised as follows:

1 They embrace a prescriptive view of language which manifests itself in a concern with grammatical correct-

ness, accurate spelling and punctuation, and neat handwriting. Pedagogically, such a view would be accompanied by regular tests and exercises in the correct forms with a heavy reliance on memorisation as a learning procedure, and on copying and dictation. A comic version of such prescriptivism is the witty remark of Keith Waterhouse (novelist, journalist, playwright and member of the Kingman Committee) that he would die a happy man if the Kingman Committee could prevent his greengrocer from putting apostrophes in potato's, tomato's, orange's and so on.

2 They believe that language can and should be stabilised and codified as a series of rules to be followed and to be taught accordingly.

3 They have an essentially ahistorical view of language and social reality. The above concern with order and organisation also represents a resistance to change in language. This in turn leads to a static, synoptic, product–centred perspective regarding language and language use. The position is particularly well characterised in the study by Milroy and Milroy (1991) entitled *Authority in Language*. Connected with this is a general lack of tolerance of linguistic variation, including dialectal variation, and a commitment to the idea of a single homogeneous *standard* English. Given that written English is generally more resistant to change, there is a pedagogical focus on writing development, and on acquisition of written norms; there is much less attention given to oral competence and oracy in general.

The Newbolt Report (DES, 1921) is particularly reactionary, as can be seen from the quotations below. We should also note that a resistance to change and a desire for linguistic homogeneity (irrespective of the facts of diversity) simultaneously embodies a *socially* reactionary adherence to keeping things the way they are. Views of language and views of social reality are never very far apart, but, above all, this position is worth noting for it is one which is particularly markedly at odds with the social philosophies of educationists who embrace romantic views of the nature of English teaching.

> We state what appears to us to be an incontrovertible primary fact, that for English children no form of knowledge can take precedence over a knowledge of English, no form of literature can take precedence over English Literature: and that the two are so inextricably connected as to form the only basis possible for a national education.

> [There should be] . . . systematic training in the use of standard English, to secure clearness and correctness both in oral expression and in writing.

> In France, we are told, this pride in the national language is strong and universal . . . such feeling for our own native language would be a bond of union between classes, and would beget the right kind of national pride. Even more certainly should pride and joy in the national literature serve as such a bond.

> (DES, 1921: 14–22)

For further discussion see, in particular, entries for **language change, national** and **proper**

Examination of a more romantic curricular philosophy of English teaching reveals an alternative view. An archetypal expression of this is in the following extract from a widely cited book by Peter Medway:

> English is about working on the knowledge we have acquired from the unsystematic processes of living, about giving expression to it and making it into a firmer and more conscious kind of knowledge. This is done through language, expressive and informal language in the first place, and eventually language akin to that of literature. Our students work through language on their own knowledge, and also gain access to other people's knowledge by way of their language, that is, through literature: we learn from literature in something like the way we do from working over our own experience.

The fact that it is literature that provides the model for the expression of knowledge in English, brings us to another of the distinctive features of that knowledge. A chemistry teacher embarking on a topic with a class will usually be able to specify what the detailed content of the work will be and what learning is expected to result. For the English teacher, the detailed content, since a large part of it will come from the students, is unpredictable, and so, therefore, is the resulting learning. But quite apart from the unpredictability, even if English teachers wanted to specify the knowledge they hoped would result, they would be unable to. The sort of knowledge that is involved is not specifiable. That is why there are no English textbooks – in the sense of books which lay out the knowledge which the subject is centrally about. Other teachers can give a statement of what they want the students to know: the task then is, in a sense, to make that statement into a psychological awareness in the student. But what students end up knowing as a result of their English work, about, say people's motivations, could never be set out as a series of propositions; instead, it would have to be revealed by the way, for instance, they handle characters in their stories. The knowledge can only be displayed by being brought to bear on particular real or imagined situations – as happens in literature.

Thus the knowledge which is handled in English is of a different kind from that which is explicitly taught in the other subjects and enshrined in their formulas, facts and texts.

(Medway, 1980: 7–8)

This quotation illustrates a number of points about romanticism:

1 A subject with no knowledge content
English is a subject without any specifiable content. In English lessons there is no knowledge to be imparted to children; instead children come to the knowledge of their

own accord, as it were. If the knowledge had to be quantified, then it would have to be by reference to experiential knowledge, the development of a knowledge of life. The pedagogic outcomes of such a position are a widespread refusal to contemplate too rigid or prescriptive a syllabus for English.

2 English as an art not a science

English is by definition opposed to science. Science is seen as dealing with facts and, therefore, as having a determinable knowledge content. Scientific subjects are seen as essentially mechanistic and anti-creative. (This is, of course, a fallacious view of science, which is a process of creative hypothesis-building and hypothesis modification with no ultimately verifiable 'facts'; however, such is the view of science adopted by many English specialists.) This view of English explains the reluctance of English teachers to develop 'language across the curriculum' projects of the kind proposed by the Bullock Report (DES, 1975). Most English teachers unconsciously resist the notion that they should in any way assume a servicing role, especially to scientific subjects.

3 Anti-formalisation

Related to both the above positions is an opposition to technicality or formalisation. There is often a strong aversion to what is seen as the 'metalanguage' or jargon of linguistics and language-based discussion. (This is an untenable position since English literary studies are redolent with terms such as rhyme, iambic pentameter, omniscient narrator, and the like. This is a simple case of metalanguages being naturalised in one's own subject area – jargon is always somebody else's jargon – but this does not mean that anti-formalisation is not a very prevalent attitude among English teachers.) Rules, technical terms and the like are associated with scientific discourse and are to be avoided lest they impose 'mind-forged manacles' on children and possibly hinder their personal growth. Such avoidance suggests some reasons for the lack of enthusiasm for the teaching of grammar with its associated rules and terminologies.

4 Individualism

Individuals and individualism are central to romantic ideologies. As the reference to 'mind-forged manacles' in the previous section demonstrates (a much-used quotation from the romantic poet, William Blake), there should be no conformity to rules or to the requirements of a social organisation and especially so if that social organisation is in any way connected with commercial or business interests. Individual pupils cannot be in any way constrained as individuals. They must not become cogs in a production line.

The pedagogic outcomes of the general positions outlined in 3 and 4 above, are as follows: an emphasis on creative writing, rather than on pre-formulation; a concern for children to write in their own words, and to choose the language and forms they require for individual expression. There will be greater attention to writing as a process in which there is minimal structural intervention by a teacher. Such pedagogies are essentially child-centred, with children making their own meanings as individual creative beings, and as far as possible, in their own words. The possible dangers of 'childism' inherent in this particular position are outlined in Martin, 1989.

5 Dualism of language and meaning

The strong belief in this connection is again an essentially romantic one. It is that language is preceded by content; that is, ideas originate independently of forms of expression and ultimately shape the choices of language and form needed to convey those ideas. In this view, then, language is only a channel, a conduit for the transmission of meanings. Such a view manifests itself in metaphors such as: *put into words*; *get your thoughts across*; *the statement was impenetrable*; *the sentence was filled with emotion*. Ideas are objects and words are merely the containers for them. Language is thus packed with ideas and sent down the conduit to a hearer.

The pedagogic consequence here is an emphasis in teaching on *what* is said, rather than on how it is said. Individually distinctive content takes precedence over the linguistic organisation and structuring of content. This view of a dualism of language and meaning leads to classroom practices which presume that students who have difficulties with writing are actually struggling to make sense of content, rather than struggling to develop the language necessary to achieve an appropriate mastery of that content.

6 Independence of language and cognition

Many teachers share the attitudes of the wider community in this regard, viewing students' mental capacities and abilities as independent from the patterns of language in which these abilities are expressed. There is a tendency to look *beyond* or *past* language, as it were; teachers tend to imagine that independently-operating cognitive abilities control the ways students perform in school, and that these abilities by their nature cannot change. There is a clear connection here with the previous observation concerning the relationship between language and content; the pedagogic outcome is a reluctance to provide pupils with the linguistic means to undertake particular cognitive tasks. Those pupils who can do it, it is assumed, are able to do so because they can do it, not because they have or have not got the means to do it.

7 Literature as a resource

Ezra Pound argued that literature was a way of keeping words living and accurate: English teachers, too, are concerned with the emotional, imaginative and 'spiritual' development of the pupil. They are engaged in exploring and manipulating the blossoming inter-dependence of reading, talking, listening and writing:

> Reading, writing, talking about writing and talking in order to write, must be continual possibilities: they overlap and interlock . . . The confidence in the modes of language which good teachers of English generate in their pupils, enables them to 'know' the world and themselves more completely. Kafka commented:
> 'A book or a poem must be an ice-axe to break the sea frozen inside us.'
> If you accept the fundamental truth beyond this startling

135

image, it is clear that English is deeply concerned with the aesthetic, the creative and the spiritual. Moreover, we are responsible for helping to develop within pupils the ability to participate sympathetically and constructively in society. This must involve an understanding of political, social and ethical issues and, most importantly, the ability to 'use' languages with confidence – in order to learn, communicate and exploit life to its full.

(Smith, 1982: 43)

The centrality of literature as a resource is the cornerstone of the romantic philosophy in so far as it affects the English classroom. Indeed, as Williams (1983) reminds us in *Keywords*, the use of the term 'literature' is a romantic invention which is still prevalent today. In the eighteenth century, the word was used to refer to writing in the broadest sense of the word: diaries, essays, travelogues, etc. The sense is retained today in phrases such as travel or insurance 'literature'. Its romantic, nineteenth-century meaning is of texts highly valued for their originality and creativity, and for their expression of a unique vision. It can be seen that the high value placed on literariness in writing affects the kind of writing which pupils are expected to produce in schools, and which is, in turn, positively regarded by many English teachers.

Literature, then, is a medium in which feeling and imagination find expression; it is also a repository of values greatly prized for their potential civilising effects. It is a resource beyond the merely functional, instrumental and utilitarian. It is instead a resource for the development of imaginative, emotional, spiritual and even moral capacities. Above all, literature fosters a critical perspective on existing social and ideological practices. Powerful literary texts are, either implicitly or explicitly, profoundly critical of societal structures, and of the value systems which support or are, in turn, supported by them. And the word 'critical' here embraces both positive and negative senses.

The pedagogies which result from this view of the centrality of literature will not be difficult to discern. They include: a limited generic range of writing in the English classroom, and a corresponding paucity of engagement with non-literary discourses. A marked focus is on the writing of stories and of narratives of personal experience in particular. At more advanced levels, the institutionalisation of the subject, for example, at 'A' level, is that of a study of literary texts. (In the 'A' level curriculum, predictably, one of the most popular papers is 'English Literature 1790–1830: English Romantic Poets'.) However, the interest in knowledge about language has led to a parallel growth in 'A' level English Language courses which offer a basis for a middle ground between the romantic and reactionary camps by attention to language structure alongside attention to language use for creative, social and cultural purposes.

The terms 'romantic' and 'reactionary' have been treated in some detail here because they are discourses in which particular ideologies have been invested and which are of considerable significance for understanding the broad parameters of contemporary debates on language and literacy. Although the terms are distinct, their distinctness should not obscure the fact that certain forms of liberal romanticism can be adhered to with reactionary zeal and that there is a certain romanticism in the nostalgia of many reactionaries for some idyllic, pastoral version of literacy practices in which teaching and learning were simply part of an ordered, uniform, 'traditional' and unproblematic process.

See also **author(ship), complaint tradition, genre, grammar, language change, literature, national, personal growth, process and product, proper**
Further reading Gilbert, 1989, 1990; Martin, 1989

S

Shakespeare   The work of the poet and dramatist William Shakespeare (1564–1616) is central to discourses about English as a subject for teaching and learning. Shakespeare is institutionalised in a range of social contexts, from syllabuses to tourist brochures, as the national poet of England. Shakespeare is regarded as the high point of high culture in England, the representative of 'the best of our past' and the purveyor of meanings and values which are universal and timeless. But Shakespeare is also contested in both right-wing and left-wing educational discourses, and his writings are appropriated for a range of political purposes.

In the National Curriculum for English in England and Wales, Shakespeare is a compulsory subject in the literature curriculum. The government has insisted on this prominence, in spite of views to the contrary, and has required that the study of Shakespeare should be accompanied by tests, of plot and of word and phrase meaning, which are more traditional in character. For example:

> Mercutio (who is dying) refers to himself as a 'grave man'. What two meanings does he expect the listeners to understand?
>
>   (DES, 1993, English, Key Stage 3, Tier 5–7)

The pervasive endorsement of Shakespeare in right-wing

discourses is not unconnected with a view of the necessary discipline required to study Shakespeare. The discipline is that of learning and remembering facts about the play and its language, a language considerably removed from present-day English. The endorsement is also founded on a belief that exposure to the greatest writing can do nothing but improve the appreciation and use of the language by students themselves. Above all, however, Shakespeare expresses 'our' culture, a national heritage of white Anglo-Saxon culture and of undoubted literary achievement, a culture of unity and hegemony to be studied and valued against the background of a contemporary Britain of ever increasing national pluralism, ethnic difference and cultural fragmentation. In such discourses Shakespeare is an icon of stable, unchanging value.

In many left-wing discourses Shakespeare is appropriated in order to be relativised, to be studied alongside poets, dramatists, pamphleteers of the Elizabethan age who are judged to be of merit, but who have not been iconised or nationalised within the institutions of the country. Indeed, for many such a broader contextual study is the main pedagogic plank in a fuller appreciation of Shakespeare's particular achievement. Such a focus also allows students to understand the cultural politics by which writers become national institutions. Additionally, Shakespeare's plays are also mined for themes and images which show his profound questioning of the established order of kingship, colonialism, the role of women in society, inherited wealth, and so on.

A more balanced position would seek to explore Shakespeare from the positions of both cultural heritage and cultural analysis, to study the plays within and outside their historical contexts of production, and to develop pedagogies which focus not simply on the words on the page, but on the ways in which the page is moved to the stage. Most teachers in Britain regret the exploitation of Shakespeare for extreme political ends, while recognising that culture and politics cannot be so simply disentangled. They regret, in particular, a government-driven, extremely traditionalist and conservative approach to testing which restricts opportunities in the class-room for challenging, imaginative engagement with the texts of Shakespeare.

See also **canon, culture, literature**
Further reading Drakakis (ed.), 1985; Easthope, 1991; Gibson, 1994

spelling

Spelling out success

Ten out of ten for Gillian Shephard! We rejoice over the Education Secretary's grand plan to teach children as young as five to spell.

She is demolishing the popular god of 'self expression' which has come close to producing a generation of illiterates.

Now there will be spelling bees and competition – another naughty word – at local and national levels.

Yes Mrs Shephard also wants schools to teach children to avoid ugly bastardised dialects.

Splendid. If she can ensure that our children can spell, add up and speak good English, she will have made the greatest contribution to education since Edward VI created the first grammar schools.

(*The Mail on Sunday*, 4 September 1994)

The teaching of spelling remains controversial. There are strong views in favour of spelling being 'caught' rather than taught; that is, exposure to the orthographic system of a language, usually through reading, is felt to be a sufficient basis for learning to spell. Views in favour of spelling being 'taught' rather than 'caught' normally presuppose teaching based on explicit spelling rules, on the memorising of word lists and on regular testing. Neither of these views in their strongest forms are soundly based. Spelling clearly has to be taught and learned in a systematic and principled way, but this does not necessarily mean that learning by rules and drills should be the exclusive means by which this is achieved.

Linguistics has been demonstrated to be of particular relevance to the teaching of spelling in the following main areas: a description of sound–symbol correspondence and of morpho-phonemic relations (the connection between individual sounds, morphemes and letter sequences); and historical semantics (the recognition of how some spelling rules are dictated by the historical origins or derivations of words).

Most teachers adopt a generally holistic and developmental view of spelling, recognising the complexities of the English spelling system at the same time as acknowledging the importance accorded to good spelling, particularly in the public domains of language use. Gentry (1982) identifies a number of developmental stages through which children pass: these stages involve recognising written symbols, that letters have sounds, that words can be abbreviated, that there are accepted strings and sequences of letters, and that these can be broken, that some words have to be learned phonetically, others by visual recall. Such stages are all transitional and indicate that learning to spell is a process and that correct spelling is not something that can be quickly delivered as a finished product. Such a developmental view demands that spelling of words such as 'ate' ('for eighty') and 'monstr' (for 'monster') are positively valued as patterned and principled stages towards the kinds of fully developed spelling competences which include a knowledge of word structure, the use of a large 'automatic' spelling vocabulary, the ability to distinguish homonyms and homophones (e.g. 'lead' (vb.) and 'lead' (n.); 'bear' and 'bare') and to distinguish grammatical and lexical structures (e.g. 'their', 'there' and 'they're') and a growing mastery of foreign loan and Latin words.

It is preferable, therefore, to regard spelling in the context of an 'emergent' literacy skill, a capacity to be gradually but systematically nurtured.

See also   **emergent literacy, process and product**
Further reading   Bissex 1980; Gentry 1982; Harris, 1993; Sampson 1985; Stubbs 1980

spoken and written language   Differences and distinctions between spoken and written language are at the root of many issues and problems in literacy development. First, the transition from a predominantly spoken competence in a language to parallel competences in spoken and written language is a key educational process; indeed success in school examinations is closely related to the development of writing abilities. Second, judgements of correctness in language are often too closely tied to judgements of correctness in the written form of the language. Third, linguistic descriptions of English as a language and of many other world languages have until very recently been based almost exclusively on written examples. One consequence of these three not unrelated facts is a certain circularity whereby high cultural and social value is placed on a written version of the language, whereby the term 'literacy' is almost synonymous with proficiency in written language and whereby key definitions of what is the standard language, what is correct and proper and even what is grammar are based on what has been described and codified in the written language. It is also worth noting here that many of the most canonical writers in the English language, such as Charles Dickens and Elizabeth Gaskell, have had difficulty in properly representing the spoken language. In their novels, such characters as are accorded the distinction of speaking the language in its most informal or dialectal forms are invariably depicted as 'illiterate', as uneducated, as unintelligent or, at best, as simply idiosyncratic.

There are several reasons for this situation. One obvious reason is that until very recently only the written forms of the language were available for detailed scrutiny. Even now very sophisticated technology is required to collect appropriate examples of spoken data. Written language is simply more available and collectable. This is one of the reasons why the

143

history of linguistics has been, until the advent of discourse analysis in the late 1970s and 1980s, the history of the study of written language systems. It is one of the reasons why the established and widely referenced grammar of the English language, *A Comprehensive Grammar of the English Language* (Quirk *et al.*, 1985), draws its 1.5 million word corpus mainly from written texts; what limited spoken data it has are based on relatively easily recordable conversations between university dons in University of London common rooms in the 1960s. Descriptions of the grammar of English depend therefore on a relatively formal restricted code but such a code is nonetheless employed as a basis for definitions of what is standard English grammar.

The following examples are of a 'spoken grammar', that is, examples of forms which are correct Standard English, which do not normally figure in grammars of the English language and which would not normally be used in most written contexts:

The man with the loud voice he said . . .
(left–displaced subject with recapitulatory pronoun 'he')

She was an outstanding leader was Mrs Gandhi.
(right–displaced subject with amplificatory noun phrase tag 'was Mrs Gandhi')

Jill likes the rock group, myself the folk.
(elliptical phrase)

That house in Brentford Street, is that where they live?
(fronted anticipatory phrase)

Several of these forms even require special descriptive labels (because the existing grammatical labels are insufficient). The existence of these examples of spoken grammar illustrates the paradox of correct spoken forms which are somehow not legitimised as correct. A major task for applied linguists and teachers is to describe the continua which exist between spoken and written versions of the language, to develop pedagogies which support pupils' transitions along and across such continua and which do not in the process either devalue the spoken or unduly privilege the written.

See also **intonation, oracy**
Further reading Chafe, 1986; Halliday, 1989; Hammond, 1990; Kress, 1993; Perera, 1992; Stubbs, 1987

Standard English

> To be unable to write Standard English or to use its spoken forms in appropriate public contexts is to be disenfranchised, to be deprived of true citizenship . . . Where it is appropriate to use the standard, you use it but there are many uses where other forms, or other languages, are as appropriate . . . It is astonishing to reflect that no linguistic theory has even begun to pose the question of the permissible range of variation within a standard although it is obvious even from the history of English that the range is not fixed.
>
> (McCabe, 1990: 11)

Standard English may be defined as that variety of English which is usually used in print and which is normally taught in schools and to non-native speakers using the language. It is also the variety which is normally spoken by educated people and used in news broadcasts and other similar situations. It is especially characterised by a rich and extensive vocalulary developed over centuries for a range of functions.

There is a particular relationship between Standard English and written forms not just in Great Britain but internationally. Its grammar and vocabulary have been codified. It is used extensively in education, including formal, public written examinations in all subjects. Beyond school, it is used widely in public and professional life. In this respect, many mother-tongue curriculum documents stress the entitlement of pupils to Standard English: not to give access to Standard English would be to disempower pupils socially and culturally. Other countries also have a Standard English. For example, there is Standard American English and Standard Australian English.

Standard English and spoken language

For some pupils, Standard English is a native dialect, that is, they are brought up speaking it. This group is not restricted geographically, and speakers of Standard English do not necessarily reveal their geographical origins in the grammar or vocabulary of their speech. Some speakers of Standard English speak it with the accent termed 'received pronunciation' (RP) or with an accent approximating to it. This accent has its origins in the variety of English spoken in public schools and within the professions and the media. It is the basis on which English pronunciation is often taught internationally. Standard English can, however, be spoken with any accent.

It is important to stress that in Great Britain today nearly all dialects are readily understood if they are spoken clearly. Standard English will be one of the most familiar, owing to its intensive media use.

A brief case study: writing and Standard English

An example of some of the complexities concerning Standard English and its functions can be provided by the piece of writing below by an eleven-year-old girl from South Yorkshire.

A Dead Pidgin
To day at afternoon play just when we was comeing back in to school Mrs B found a pidgin on the floor next to the Haygreen Lane side. Some children had gone in but I was ther when Gary Destains said hay up thers a pidgin on floor. We all rusht up but Mrs B showted 'stop come back and let me look whats apened to it poor thing.' I just thout it was resting a bit but Dobbie said its ded. It was when Mrs B picket it up its kneck just flopped over poor thing I

said to Dobbie. She lifted it up with its wings and they were like big lovley grey fans. I didn't know wings were so lovely and big with so meny feathers espechily. When we had gon in we was just sittin in are class and telling Mrs Sandison and the others about it when Mrs B came and held it up with its lovely grey wings. I was sorry for it poor thing and Mrs Sandison was sad and we all was.

Lesley, year 5

A teacher working with Lesley on this piece of writing cannot simply 'correct' it; instead most teachers would view the writing as a process and work with Lesley to help her understand the purposes of different types and varieties of English.

As far as spelling is concerned, the writer can be given the correct Standard English orthography for some words (e.g. *many*, *gone*, *coming*, *there*, *there's* are frequent words and need to be known); other words need to be seen more developmentally, as part of an emergent view of appropriate spelling (indeed, words like *espechily*, *pidgin*, *kneck* show a familiarity with basic spelling patterns in English which should be viewed positively in a progression towards learning the correct forms). Other words are, however, less clear-cut, for Lesley transcribes a number of words and phrases based on her pronunciation of them in her South Yorkshire accent (for example *whats apened* – 'what's *h*appened' in Standard English; *hay up* which has no automatic equivalent in Standard English dialect).

With regard to these overlaps between spoken transcription and standard forms a further major point about the whole piece of writing is that Lesley divided her account into two main sections: a section which describes the events and a section in which dialogue occurs. Accordingly, it would be important for the teacher to help Lesley distinguish between local dialect uses in the description and in the dialogue. In the first case, examples such as *we was comeing* and *we all was* are not appropriate to formal third-person narrative description; in the second case, the writer should have the option of retaining them to give authenticity to the record of speech and

147

may thus have greater freedom in how this speech is to be spelled.

Standard English and appropriacy

> At the centre of the new orthodoxy is its devaluation of standard English. From this derives its exponent's hostility to grammatical prescription: *because* they do not think that standard English is superior to dialect, they do not believe that its grammar should be prescribed to children . . . *because* they cannot accept that standard English is superior to dialect, they insist that the language schoolchildren use can be judged only by its 'appropriateness'.
>
> (Marenbon, 1987)

Though it has been extensively described and codified, Standard English is not an homogeneous entity; it is subject to historical change and variation across the world. Standard English has many sub-varieties. For example, Standard Scientific English, Standard Medical English, and Standard Business English are all different from each other, and there are different varieties of Business English, some formal and legalistic, some technical, some persuasive, which are used on different occasions and for different purposes. There are contexts in which Standard Spoken English is appropriate and desirable (for example, in most formal interview situations, or in public discourse with larger, unknown audiences); but there are other situations in which formal Standard English may be out of place (such as small group discussions with colleagues or friends), in which more informal, local dialect forms may be more appropriate – as long as communication is clear and comprehensible.

However, the key word 'standard' itself must also be interrogated. On one level it is connected, of course, with proper and correct notions of language. There is also, however, especially in the discourses of many politicians and their media allies, a constant slippage from the word 'standard' to educational, moral and social standards. Here is an example provided by a former Chairman of the British Conservative Party:

> we've allowed so many standards to slip . . . teachers weren't bothering to teach kids to spell and to punctuate properly . . . if you allow standards to slip to the stage where good English is no better than bad English, where people turn up filthy . . . at school . . . all those things cause people to have no standards at all, and once you lose standards then there's no imperative to stay out of crime.
>
> (Norman Tebbit, Radio 4, 1985)

To uphold standard English is to uphold standards. The connection here between standards of English and standards of hygiene is also revealing. Standard English is a mark of purity and cleanliness, while non-standard English is unclean. This is almost as revealing as the sequence of logical non-sequiturs which lead to Lord Tebbit's equation of illiteracy and crime.

The term 'standard' itself inevitably causes problems in discussions of language. In one sense it can mean uniform, ordinary, common to all, and normal. In this sense it carries the meaning of 'standard' measure, as in a standard British weight or nail or plug. In a second sense, 'standard' means a sign or sculptured figure or flag of a particular power, usually a political power – a king, a noble or a commander – as in a ship's standard or the Queen's standard or in the term 'standard-bearer' – something around which could be grouped armies, fleets, nations and cities. The senses also now converge in the meaning of standard as authoritative so that Standard English becomes the common, standard language used by those in authority. The standard becomes thus no longer a marker for an authority external to it but an authority in itself. The standard language is language with a standard and the normative is reinforced as the normal. The whole process illustrates the unambiguous connection between standard language and social and political power and helps to explain the much-quoted statement that any standard language is no more than a dialect with an army and a navy.

In the history of the English language such a process accelerated during the eighteenth century in particular, coinciding with the growth of a centralised nation state linguistically based on the East Midlands dialect of the South-East of the country, and reinforced with a central-to-region administration centred in metropolitan London.

Further interrogation of 'standard' as a keyword occurs in Raymond Williams's *Keywords* (1983), in which he isolates additional meanings to the word such as 'standard' model (meaning basic or minimum specification) and 'gold standard' (meaning a basic unit of comparison) – meanings which further complicate the association of standard not only with what is exceptional and authoritative but also with what is measurable and specifiable. The term 'standard' is protean. It is simultaneously 'distinctive', 'correct', 'authorised', 'accepted', 'ordinary', 'superior', 'measurable'. It is perhaps not surprising that so many confusions and disagreements exists in discussion of Standard English. As the quotation from McCabe cited at the beginning of this entry illustrates, it is also confusing that the question of variation within Standard English has not been fully addressed either in theory or in practice. In other words, there are many constructions which are widely used by what would be regarded as Standard English speakers, but which have not been described as Standard English. For example, is a 'standard' spoken construction such as 'What did she say, your sister?' to be dismissed as non-standard because it does not appear in standard grammars? Or is it accepted as part of the variational range of Standard English? Such questions need much more extensive linguistic analysis, not least because there are very important implications for the teaching of Standard English.

Standard English (teaching of)   There is little disagreement that the teaching of standard written English is both necessary and desirable, though opinions will differ over appropriate supporting pedagogies, particularly the nature of a teacher's intervention in writing processes in which pupils are effecting transitions from spoken (in some cases non-standard spoken) forms to standard written forms. However, disagreement is sharper over teaching spoken Standard English and is, in fact, often confused by assumptions that there is a single correct accent for Standard English when the linguistic reality is that Standard English can be spoken in a variety of accents.

The Cox Report on English in the National Curriculum in England and Wales recommends both caution and realism in what can be expected in the use by pupils of spoken standard English at different stages of development. Nevertheless the revisions to the National Curriculum proposed in *English 5 to 16* (DES, 1993) strengthen programmes of study and attainment targets for speaking and listening in all key stages, to concentrate on enabling pupils to become 'confident' and 'articulate' users of Standard English. Michael Stubbs, drawing on recent linguistic and educational research, reminds us of some of the difficulties and complexities of such a requirement:

> It is very much more doubtful whether children should be explicitly taught spoken SE. They must be able to understand it, of course, but it is doubtful if schools should try to teach or insist on production in spoken SE. First, such an insistence is unlikely to be successful. Children know that not everyone speaks SE, and an insistence that they should speak it is likely to alienate them from the school or their family or both. In any case, the habits of the spoken language are usually so deeply ingrained that they are impervious to conscious teaching for a few hours a week in school. People need to be very highly motivated in order to change their native dialect. Writing depends much more on conscious language behaviour, and is therefore open to explicit teaching in a way in which spoken language is not.
>
> (Stubbs, 1986: 95–6)

See also **appropriate, correct, dialect, language and empowerment, non-standard (English), proper, purism, spoken and written language**

Further reading Crowley 1989; Leith 1983; McCabe 1990; Milroy and Milroy, 1991, 1993; Perera, 1984; Stubbs 1986; Wilkinson 1995

stylistics (language and literature) The subject of stylistics is not a new one. Its roots lie in research into style by literary linguists in the Moscow and Prague Philological Circles during the 1920s and 1930s, work which was developed by major figures in the field such as Leo Spitzer in the 1940s and 1950s. The institutionalisation of the subject in academic courses proceeded during the 1960s and 1970s with the result that many university departments of English Studies or Humanities now have courses entitled 'literary linguistics', 'literary language' or 'stylistics'; they apply techniques derived from linguistic analysis to what is argued to be a more than usually detailed and systematic interpretation of the part played by language in the creation of textual meanings, The marriage of linguistics and literary studies has not been without its disputes, both ideological and territorial, and there have been partings of the ways. There have been numerous recent signs, however, of increasing reconciliations and new alignments.

Much of the impetus to fuller integration can be traced to two main developments in literary linguistic studies during the late 1970s and in the 1980s: an openness to new directions in literary theory and a broadening of the parameters of analysis and discussion to include notions of *discourse*. Of these the growth in the study of discourse has been the most significant. One of the main reasons why the analysis of discourse has served a unifying role is that the domains of language and discourse are central to the study of texts and the organisation of texts.

See also **culture, discourse, English, rhetoric, text**
Further reading Carter and Nash, 1990; Widdowson, 1992; Montgomery *et al.*, 1992

T

testing/tests   Testing language and literacy development is a process by which a student's abilities, knowledge and performance can be measured. A test can be formative, providing teachers with valuable diagnostic information on which to build for future development, or evaluative, ranking students' performance relative to a set of predetermined objectives. In test-types a main distinction is drawn between criterion-referenced tests and norm-referenced tests. For criterion-referenced tests students have to reach an externally regulated level of performance; for norm-referenced tests achievement is measured relatively to other groups of comparable students rather than according to any predetermined level.

In cultural and political contexts in which schools are required to be more accountable and to compete with other schools for pupils and resources, the availability for public scrutiny of test results, particularly in key domains such as language and literacy, and the nature and extent of those results assume particular importance. The general preference of governments is for such 'objective' information to be widely published, preferably in tabulated form so that the achievements of individual schools can be appropriately calculated. The preference of teachers and schools is to be more guarded about the 'objectivity' of tests, to point out that

153

a variety of complex factors, including the nature of the intake, determine the relative success of schools and to use tests mainly for formative and diagnostic purposes. Governments also require in such contexts that tests should be increasingly set and assessed externally and be nationally uniform; teachers argue that a significant proportion of marks for tests should be provided by their own internal assessments, which should take due account of achievement over a more extended period of time than that normally allowed by external tests. They value in particular the kinds of holistic assessment in which formal, timed tests are combined with more flexible modes such as projects and related work compiled incrementally over the duration of a course.

In the National Curriculum in England and Wales, tests at 7, 11, 14 and 16 years are an integral component. Most subjects measure progress according to a ten-point scale of assessment with graded targets for different levels of attainment. One problem with such scales is that not all subjects lend themselves to measurement of achievement in a neat linear fashion; literacy development, for example, is often recursive and cyclical and the testing of reading competences is a highly complex procedure involving a range of factors that go beyond an 'objective' test of word recognition. Indeed, few decontextualised tests of reading determine anything more than an ability to read decontextualised words, whereas reading competence presupposes an ability to read for meaning which is dependent on skills of semantic and grammatical (in addition to phonetic) decoding, inferencing and on using contextual and related clues to aid comprehension.

Tests will continue to prove an ideological battleground since they serve to establish hierarchies of attainment, with success and failure clearly and publicly demarcated. The main problem for testers and the tested is not whether there should be tests but the nature of the tests, their frequency and the optimum ages at which they can be conducted.

See also **phonics, projects**

text   This is a term commonly used by linguists to refer to a complete stretch of language, either spoken or written. A one-line advertisement or headline can be a text since it is a complete semantic unit, but the practice of text analysis (also known as text linguistics) is not principally concerned with individual words or sentences. It is concerned with the way in which they combine across sentence boundaries and speaking turns to form coherently organised language in use in a specific context.

Although texts are spoken as well as written, for purposes of analysis the analyst effectively deals with a written record. It should also be recognised that the term 'text' often refers to a definable communicative unit with a clearly discernible social or cultural function. Thus a casual conversation, a sermon, a poster, a poem, or an advertisement would be referred to as texts. In some studies in this field, the terms 'text' and 'text analysis' can be interchangeable with 'discourse' and 'discourse analysis'.

The term 'text' in the sense of a unit of spoken and written material to be analysed and criticised has a particular ascendancy at present in the field of English Studies, which was previously dominated by a study of literary 'works'. Depending on one's position, the term 'text' either serves to democratise English Studies so that no one type of text is unduly privileged, or it serves to undermine the critical judgements of the past, which have established a canon of literary works deemed to be of lasting value within and beyond the national culture that produced them.

Current practice in English Studies in both secondary and tertiary sectors in many parts of the world is to question common assumptions about 'text' and to explore what is meant by words such as 'canon', 'value', 'national', 'culture' and 'judgement'. The development of text studies and text analysis has placed a key emphasis on language. It has led to the expansion of a text and discourse-based linguistics as one of the main instruments by which texts can be analysed, and to a not unfamiliar paradox within English Studies that language is at once the instrument and object of analysis.

One of the main methodological objectives of text analysis is to compare and contrast texts; this, pedagogically, serves to heighten awareness of differences and distinctions between the spoken and written, the literary and non-literary, the canonical and non-canonical, and a wide range of different text types. For some teachers the resulting awareness can also form the basis for improvements in competence in language use. The rapid expansion of upper secondary school 'A' level courses in England in English Language is predicated on assumptions that text and text analysis are central to learning in, through, and about English.

See also **canon, cohesion, critical linguistics, culture, discourse, discourse analysis, knowledge about language, language awareness, literature, rhetoric, stylistics**
Further reading Carter and Nash, 1990; Cook 1990, 1992; Easthope, 1991; Fairclough, 1992

variation (in language) Prescriptive views of language are predicated on a mono-model of language; that is, only one correct version of the language has any real significance, and other varieties or versions of the language can be discounted. Descriptive views recognise that variation is fundamental to language. Language varies according to the purposes for which it is used, according to the contexts in which it is used, and according to the people by whom and with whom it is used. Language also changes over time, so that the forms of the language differ from one generation to another.

Variation over time is referred to as *diachronic* variation; variation according to the individual or group who uses it is termed *dialectal* variation, and variation according to uses and purposes is termed *diatypic* variation. For example, changes in language over time are regularly the result of socio-cultural or socio-economic changes. From the mid-seventeenth to the nineteenth century the growth of the East Midlands dialect into the standard English dialect of Great Britain and subsequently internationally too, can be attributed largely to the economic and political power of London and to the social attitudes which associate with such power, particularly in respect of the connection of 'non-standard' dialects with other geographical locations.

Contemporary uses of dialect forms are also often directly

157

dependent on the social position of the user and on his or her attitudes towards it. A whole body of sociolinguistic research (e.g. Trudgill, 1983) confirms that dialectal variation occurs according to a range of largely socially constructed parameters. Such work also demonstrates that dialects are not fixed entities but rather continua, with users making choices along the continua according to their social status, their perception of their own and their interlocutor's social status, their assessment of the nature of the context of their language use as well as such factors as their own gender or ethnicity and their perception of their interlocator(s) in relation to such factors. Geographical factors are also relevant and for some users a sense of belonging to a particular community will be a crucial factor in choices along the continua of dialectal variation, not least because such choices will involve expressions of their identity as individuals. A further marker of individuality resides in the *idolects* which each speaker possesses, which are particular choices of words or phrases or particular phonological characteristics which single out one user from another. Such characteristics are largely regular over time. In more senses than one, however, dialectal variation reveals who you are.

Diatypic variation is also deeply embedded in different social contexts of use. A fundamental component of this variation, particularly in educational contexts, is a continuum between spoken and written *modes*. Differences and distinctions between speech and writing result in different diatypes with different communicative functions. For example, a written report is usually different from a spoken report. We need to remember, however, that different degrees of rehearsal or planning can underlie the same function within the two modes. A planned spoken report, which can even have been written to be spoken, will contain different forms of language from an unplanned one and for this main reason poles of 'planned' and 'unplanned' may be more significant than choices in spoken and written modes, however fundamental such choices are. Also significant in this variation will be the audience and the formality of the relations between the user and the audience; and the very subject-matter, as well as assumptions of familiarity with the general topic, will determine choices of mode and judgement of appropriate reception of the language. Such judgement will, of course, involve conscious or unconscious perception of the power relations which obtain in the socio-cultural context of this use of language as well as the relation of the choices of particular language forms to the ideologies, beliefs and value systems of the participants.

A final example also illustrates that the diatypic, the dialectal and the diachronic can converge. In the utterance

He shouldn't ought to do it to the bairns.

we recognise a dialect common in the North of England and particularly in Scotland. The dialect involves both grammatical difference (e.g. 'He shouldn't ought to' – Standard English 'He oughtn't to') and lexical differences ('bairns' – Standard English 'children'). The user here will, however, be more likely to speak rather than write such English, though may do so in informal contexts such as a personal letter. Furthermore, diachronically, the word 'ought' is changing in Standard British English dialect, and in many contexts 'He shouldn't do it to the children' may be more commonly found, though a further choice may be made in some formal written contexts by omitting 'shouldn't' and replacing it with 'should not'. Much depends on judgements of appropriacy for there can be no unequivocally correct rules of usage here and we should not forget that the speaker's personal identity is at all times closely bound up with the North English/Scottish forms in both grammar and vocabulary.

It is fitting that language variation should be one of the final keywords in this book. The concept of language variety embodies the 'centrifugal' tendencies in language discussed in the introductory preface. It will be understood therefore why the National Curriculum for English in England and Wales, welcomed by teachers and educationalists in the early 1990s, and which recognised the inherent variability of language,

159

is already being revised by a government concerned to give priority to centripetal forms in language.

The teaching of English, however, is recognised by most practitioners to need to take full account of linguistic variation in theory and practice. Most teachers of English will continue, therefore, to endorse the view that effective language use can only be properly measured in relation to the contexts of the user (dialect) and the contexts of the use (diatype), and that for pupils to learn to use language with clarity, purpose and confidence they need, above all, to understand the different varieties of English and the choices that accompany their use.

See also **dialect, language change, register, spoken and written language, Standard English**
Further reading Halliday and Hasan, 1989

write/writing   Discourses about writing vary in relation to perceived purposes of writing. For most teachers of English it is important for a balance between process and product to be maintained. That is, much is learned about writing and the shape of writing in relation to communicative purpose from processes of drafting and re-drafting. Teachers also realise that the construction of texts depends on writers understanding the relationship between words across sentence boundaries and the cohesive organisation of sentences. In order for children to learn such aspects of writing, many teachers of English believe it best for writing to remain person-centred for as long as possible, with writers shaping their writing according to the nature of their individual experiences.

For non-specialists and employers, success in writing is judged rather more in relation to accuracy in the secretarial aspects of writing, such as spelling and punctuation, and correctness in sentence grammar. Greater weight is given to more impersonal modes of writing, such as reports and instructions. The National Curriculum for English in England and Wales is currently being modified away from process-based approaches and towards more impersonal and secretarial features of writing, with a greater emphasis on accuracy than on fluency.

See also **authorship, cohesion, genre, process and product**
Further reading Czerniewska, 1992; Harris, 1993; Kress, 1993; Sampson, 1985; Smith, 1982

REFERENCES

Aitchison, J. (1991) *Language Change: Progress or Decay*, 2nd edn, (Cambridge University Press, Cambridge).

Alladina, S. and Edwards, V. (eds) (1991) *Multilingualism in the British Isles*, Vols I and II (London, Longman).

Andrews, R. (ed.) (1989) *Narrative and Argument* (Open University Press, Milton Keynes).

Bain, R., Fitzgerald, B. and Taylor, M. (eds) (1992) *Looking into Language: Classroom Approaches to Knowledge about Language* (Hodder & Stoughton, Sevenoaks).

Bakhtin, M. (1981) 'Discourse in the Novel', in *The Dialogic Imagination* (University of Austin Press, Austin, Tex.).

Ball, S. J. (ed.) (1990) *Foucault and Education: Disciplines and Knowledge* (Routledge, London).

Barton, D. (1994) *Literacy: an Introduction to the Ecology of Written Language* (Blackwell, Oxford).

Bauer, L. (1994) *Watching English Change* (Longman, London).

Baynham, M. (1994) *Literacy Practices: Investigating Literacy in Social Contexts* (Longman, London).

Bhaba, H. (1994) *The Location of Culture* (Routledge, London).

Bhatia, V.K. (1993) *Analyzing Genre: Language Use in Professional Settings* (Longman, London).

Birch, D. (1989) *Language, Literature and Critical Practice* (Routledge, London).

Bissex, G.L. (1980) *GNYS AT WRK: A Child Learns to Read and Write* (Harvard University Press, Cambridge, Mass.).

Bourne, J. (1989) *Moving into the Mainstream: LEA Provision for Bilingual Pupils* (London, NFER/Nelson).

Bourne, J. and Cameron D. (1989) 'No common ground: Kingman, grammar and the nation', *Language and Education*, 2 (3), pp. 147–60 .

Brazil, D. (1995) *The Grammar of Speech* (Oxford University Press, Oxford).

Brice Heath, S. (1983) *Ways with Words: Language, Life and Work in Communities and Classrooms* (Cambridge University Press, Cambridge).

Brindley, S. (ed.) *Teaching English* (Routledge, London).

Brumfit, C. J. (ed.) (1995) *Language Education in the National Curriculum* (Blackwell, Oxford).

Bruner, J. (1974) *The Relevance of Education* (Penguin, Harmondsworth).

Bruner, J. (1986) *Actual Minds, Possible Worlds* (Harvard University Press, Cambridge, Mass.).

Bygate, M. (1989) *Speaking* (Oxford University Press, Oxford).

Carter, R. (1987) *Vocabulary: Applied Linguistic Perspectives* (Routledge, London).

Carter, R. (ed.) (1990a) *Knowledge about Language and the Curriculum: The LINC Reader* (Hodder & Stoughton, Sevenoaks).

Carter, R. (1990b) 'The new grammar teaching', in R. Carter (ed.) *Knowledge about Language and the Curriculum: The LINC Reader* (Hodder & Stoughton, Sevenoaks), pp. 104–21.

Carter, R. (1991) *The National Curriculum for English: A Guide to the Development of a National Curriculum for English in England and Wales 1984–1990* (British Council, London).

Carter, R. (1993) *Introducing Applied Linguistics* (Penguin, Harmondsworth).

Carter, R. (forthcoming) 'Politics and knowledge about language', in R. Hasan and G. Williams, *Literacy in Society* (Longman, London).

Carter, R and Nash, W. (1990) *Seeing through Language: a Guide to Styles of English Writing* (Oxford, Blackwell).

Chafe, W. (1986) 'Writing in the perspective of speaking', in R. Cooper and S. Greenbaum (eds) *Studying Writing: Linguistic Approaches* (Sage, Newbury Park, California), pp. 12–39.

Christie, F. (1989) *Language Education* (Deakin University/Oxford University Press, Oxford).

Clay, M. (1972) *The Early Detection of Reading Difficulties* (Heinemann, London).

Coates, J. (1993) *Women, Men and Language*, 2nd edn (Longman, Harlow).

Coates, J. and Cameron, D. (eds) (1989) *Women in their Speech Communities* (Longman, London).

Cockroft, R. and Cockroft, S. (1992) *Rhetoric* (Macmillan, Basingstoke).

Coggle, B. (1993) *Do You Speak Estuary?* (Bloomsbury, London).

Cook, G. (1990) *Discourse* (Oxford University Press, Oxford).

Cook, G. (1992) *The Discourse of Advertising* (Routledge, London).

Cope, B. and Kalantzis, M. (eds) (1993) *The Powers of Literacy: a Genre Approach to Teaching Writing* (Falmer Press, Brighton).

Coulmas, F. (ed.) (1991) *A Language Policy for the European Community: Prospects and Quandaries* (Mouton de Gruyter, Berlin/New York).

Coulthard, M. (1985) *Introduction to Discourse Analysis*, 2nd edn (Longman, Harlow).

Cox, B. (1991) *Cox on Cox: An English Curriculum for the 1990s* (Hodder & Stoughton, Sevenoaks).

Crowley, T. (1989) *The Politics of Discourse: the Standard Language Question and British Cultural Debates* (Macmillan, London).

Crowley, T. (ed.) (1991) *Proper English? Readings in Language, History and Cultural Identity* (Routledge, London).

Crystal, D. (1985) *Who Cares About English Usage?* (Penguin, Harmondsworth).

Crystal, D. and Davy, D. (1969) *Investigating English Style* (Longman, Harlow).

Czerniewska, P. (1992) *Learning about Writing: the Early Years* (Blackwell, Oxford).

Daly, M. and English Curriculum Group (1989) 'Different views of the subject: a PGCE perspective', *The English Magazine*, 22, pp. 15–17.

DES (1921) *The Teaching of English in England: Being the Report of the Committee Appointed by the President of the Board of Education to Inquire into the Position of English in the Education System of England* (The Newbolt Report) (HMSO, London).

DES (1975) *A Language For Life* (The Bullock Report) (HMSO, London).

DES (1984) *English 5 to 16: Curriculum Matters 1* (NCC/HMSO, London).

DES (1985) *Education for All* (The Swann Report) (HMSO, London).

DES (1986) *English 5 to 16: Curriculum Matters 2* (NCC/HMSO, London).

DES (1988) *Report of the Committee of Inquiry into the Teaching of English Language* (The Kingman Report) (HMSO, London).

DES (1989) *Report of the English Working Party 5 to 16* (The Cox Report) (HMSO, London).

DES (1993) *English 5 to 16: Responses to Curriculum Matters 1* (HMSO, London).

Dixon, J. (1975) *Growth Through English* (Oxford University Press, Oxford).

Dixon, J. and Stratta, L. (1992) 'The National Curriculum in English: does genre theory have anything to offer?'. *English in Education* 26 (2), pp. 16–27.

Donmall, G. (ed.) (1985) *Language Awareness* (Centre for Information on Language Teaching, London).

Doyle, B (1989) *English and Englishness* (Routledge, London).

Drakakis, J. (ed.) (1985) *Alternative Shakespeares* (Routledge, London).

Easthope, A. (1991) *Literary into Cultural Studies* (Routledge, London).

Edwards, A. and Westgate, D. P. G. (1987) *Investigating Classroom Talk* (Falmer Press, Brighton).

Edwards, V. (1979) *The West Indian Language Issue in British Schools* (Batsford, London).

Elley, W. B. *et al.* (1975) 'The role of grammar in a secondary school English curriculum', *New Zealand Journal of Educational Research*, 10 (1), pp. 26–42.

Evans, C. (1993) *English People* (Open University Press, Milton Keynes).

Fairclough, N. (1989) *Language and Power* (Longman, London).

Fairclough, N. (1992) *Discourse and Social Change* (Polity Press, Cambridge).

Fairclough, N. (ed.) (1993) *Critical Language Awareness* (Longman, London).

Fishman, T. (1981) 'Language policy: past, present and future', in C.A. Ferguson and S. Brice Heath (eds) *Language in the USA* (Cambridge University Press, Cambridge).

Fox, C. (1993) *At the Very Edge of the Forest: the Influence of Literature on Storytelling* (Cassell, London).

Freire, P. and Macedo, D. (1987) *Literacy: Reading the Word and the World* (Routledge, London).

Gannon, P. (1985) *Assessing Language* (Edward Arnold, London).

Garton, A. and Pratt, C. (1989) *Learning to be Literate* (Blackwell, Oxford).

Gee, J. (1990) *Social Linguistics and Literacies: Ideology in Discourses* (Falmer Press, London).

Gentry, M. (1982) 'An analysis of developmental spelling in GNYS AT WORK', *Reading Teacher*, 36, pp. 192–200.

Gibson, R. (1994) 'Teaching Shakespeare in schools', in S. Brindley (ed.) *Teaching English* (Routledge, London), pp. 140–8.

Gilbert, P. (1989) *Writing, Schooling and Disadvantage: from Voice to Text in the Classroom* (Routledge, London).

Gilbert, P. (1990) 'Authorizing disadvantage: authorship and creativity in the language classroom', in F. Christie (ed.) *Literacy for a Changing World* (Australian Council for Educational Research, Hawthorn, Victoria), pp. 54–78.

Goodman, K. (1982) *Language and Literacy: the Selected Writings of Kenneth Goodman* (Routledge, London).

Goodson, I. and Medway, P. (eds) (1990) *Bringing English to Order: the History and Politics of a School Subject* (Falmer Press, Brighton).

Graddol, D. and Swan, J. (1989) *Gender Voices* (Blackwell, Oxford).

Graves, D. (1983) *Writing: Teachers and Children at Work* (Heinemann, London).

Griffiths, P. (1992) *English at the Core: Dialogue and Power in English Teaching* (Open University Press, Milton Keynes).

Hall, N. (1987) *The Emergence of Literacy* (Hodder & Stoughton, Sevenoaks).

Halliday M. A. K. (1987) 'Some basic concepts in educational linguistics', in V. Bickley (ed.) *Languages in Education in a Bi-lingual or Multi-lingual Setting* (ILE, Hong Kong), pp. 5–17.

Halliday, M. A. K. (1989) *Spoken and Written Language* (Oxford University Press, Oxford).

Halliday, M. A. K. (1990) 'Linguistic perspectives on literacy: a systemic-functional approach', mimeo, University of Sydney, Department of Linguistics.

Halliday, M. A. K. and Hasan, R. (1989) *Language, Context and Text* (Oxford University Press, Oxford).

Hamilton, M., Barton, D. and Ivanic, R. (eds) (1994) *Worlds of Literacy* (Multilingual Matters, Clevedon, Avon).

Hammond, J. (1990) 'Is learning to read the same as learning to speak?', in F. Christie (ed.) *Literacy for a Changing World* (Australian Council for Educational Research, Sydney) pp. 26–53.

Hardy, B. (1968) 'Towards a poetics of fiction', reprinted as 'The narrative imagination' in B. Hardy, *Tellers and Listeners* (Athlone Press, London, 1975).

Harris, R. J. (1962) 'An experimental inquiry into the functions and values of formal grammar in the teaching of English', Ph.D. thesis, University of London.

Harris, J. (1993) *Introducing Writing* (Penguin, Harmondsworth).

Harris, J. and Wilkinson, J. (1986) *Reading Children's Writing* (Routledge, London).

Hasan, R. and Williams, G. (eds) (forthcoming) *Literacy in Society* (Longman, London).

Hawkins, E. (1987) *The Awareness of Language*, rev. edn (Cambridge University Press, Cambridge).

Hayhoe, S. and Parker, S. (eds) (1994) *Who Owns English?* (Open University Press, Milton Keynes).

Honey, J. (1989) *Does Accent Matter?* (Faber, London).

Hudson, R. (1991) *Teaching Grammar: A Guide for the National Curriculum* (Blackwell, Oxford).

James, C. and Garrett, P. (eds) (1991) *Language Awareness in the Classroom* (Longman, Harlow).

Johnson, J. (1994) 'The National Oracy Project', in S. Brindley (ed.) *Teaching English* (Routledge, London), pp. 33–42.

Keen, J. (1992) *Language and the English Curriculum* (Open University Press, Milton Keynes).

Kramsch, C. (1993) *Context and Culture in Language Teaching* (Oxford University Press, Oxford).

Kress, G. (1989) *Linguistic Processes in Sociocultural Practice* (Oxford University Press, Oxford).

Kress, G. (1993) *Learning to Write*, 2nd edn (Routledge, London).

Labov, W. (1972) *Language in the Inner City* (University of Philadelphia Press, Philadelphia, Pa.).

Lee, D. (1992) *Competing Discourses: Perspectives and Ideology in Language* (Longman, London).

Legutke, M. and Thomas, H. (1991) *Process and Experience in the Language Classroom* (Longman, London).

Leith, D. (1983) *A Social History of English* (Routledge, London).

LINC (1992) *Language in the National Curriculum (LINC): Materials for Professional Development* (University of Nottingham, Department of English Studies).

Littlefair, A. (1992) *Reading All Types of Writing* (Open University Press, Milton Keynes).

LMP (Linguistic Minorities Project) (1985) *The Other Languages of England* (Routledge, London).

Luke, A. (1988) *Literacy, Textbooks and Ideology* (Falmer Press, London).

168

Macaulay, W.J. (1947) 'The difficulty of grammar', *British Journal of Educational Psychology*, 17, pp. 153–62.

Marenbon, J. (1987) *English, Our English: The New Orthodoxy Examined* (Centre for Policy Studies, London).

Martin, J. (1989) *Factual Writing: Exploring and Challenging Social Reality* (Oxford University Press, Oxford).

Maybin, J. (ed.) (1993) *Language and Literacy in Social Practice* (Multilingual Matters, Clevedon).

McCabe, C. (1990) 'Language, literature, identity: reflections on the Cox Report', *Critical Quarterly*, 32 (4), p. 11.

McCarthy, M. (1991) *Discourse Analysis for Language Teachers* (Cambridge University Press, Cambridge).

McCarthy, M. and Carter, R. (1994) *Language as Discourse: Perspectives for Language Teaching* (Longman, Harlow).

Medway, P. (1980) *Finding a Language: Autonomy and Learning in School* (Chameleon Books, London).

Meek, M. (1988) *How Texts Teach What Readers Learn* (Thimble Press, Oxford).

Meek, M. and Mills, C. (eds) (1989) *Language and Literacy in the Primary School* (Falmer Press, London).

Miller, J. (1983) *Many Voices* (Routledge, London).

Milroy, J. and Milroy, L. (1991) *Authority in Language*, 2nd edn (Routledge, London).

Milroy, J. and Milroy, L. (1993) *Real English: the Grammar of English Dialects in the British Isles* (Longman, London).

Montgomery, M., Durant, A., Fabb, N., Furniss, T. and Mills, S. (1992) *Ways of Reading* (Routledge, London).

Moss, G. (1989) *Un/Popular Fictions* (Virago, London).

Nash, W. (1986) *English Usage* (Routledge, London).

Nash, W. (1989) *Rhetoric: the Wit of Persuasion* (Blackwell, Oxford).

Norman, K. (ed.) (1992) *Thinking Voices: the Work of the National Oracy Project* (Hodder & Stoughton, Sevenoaks).

Nunan, D. (1993) *Introducing Discourse Analysis* (Penguin, Harmondsworth).

Perera, K. (1984) *Children's Writing and Reading* (Blackwell, Oxford).

Perera, K. (1990) 'Grammatical differentiation between speech and writing in children aged 8–12', in R. A. Carter (ed.) *Knowledge about Language and the Curriculum: the LINC Reader* (Hodder & Stoughton, Sevenoaks), pp. 216–33.

Perera, K. (1993) 'Standard English in Attainment Target 1: Speaking and Listening', *Language Matters* (Centre for Language in Primary Education), no. 3, p. 10.

Quirk, R., Greenbaum, S., Leech, G. and Svartvik, J. (1985) *A Comprehensive Grammar of the English Language* (Longman, Harlow).

Rae, J. (1982) 'The decline and fall of English grammar', *Observer*, 7 February.

Reid, I. (ed.) (1987) *The Place of Genre in Learning: Current Debates* (Deakin University Press, Geelong, Victoria).

Richards, J., Platt, J and Weber, H. (1993) *Longman Dictionary of Applied Linguistics*, 2nd edn (Longman, Harlow).

Richmond, J. (1982) *The Resources of Classroom Language* (Edward Arnold, London).

Richmond, J. (1990) 'What do we mean by "knowledge about language"' in R. A. Carter (ed.) *Knowledge about Language and the Curriculum* (Hodder & Stoughton, Sevenoaks), pp. 23–44.

Richmond, J. (1992) 'Unstable materials', *The English Magazine*, 26, pp. 13–18.

Rockhill, J. (1993) 'Gender, language and the politics of literacy', in J. Maybin (ed.) *Language and Literacy in Social Practice* (Multilingual Matters, Clevedon), pp. 233–51.

Romaine, S. (1984) *Pidgin and Creole Languages* (Longman, London).

Rosen, H. (1988) 'Responding to Kingman' in E. Ashworth, and L. Masterman (eds) *Responding to Kingman*, University of Nottingham (mimeo).

Rost, M. (1994) *Introducing Listening* (Penguin, Harmondsworth).

Said, E. (1976) *Orientalism* (Penguin, Harmondsworth).

Said, E. (1994) *Culture and Imperialism* (Faber, London).

Sampson, G. (1985) *Writing Systems* (Hutchinson, London).

Scollon, R. and Scollon, S. (1981) *Narrative, Literacy and Face in Interethnic Communication* (Ablex, Norwood, NJ).

Sebba, M. (1993) *London Jamaican: a Case Study in Language Interaction* (Longman, London).

Simpson, P. (1993) *Language, Ideology and Point of View* (Routledge, London).

Smith, F. (1982) *Writing and the Writer* (Heinemann, London).

Smith, F. (1985) *Reading*, 2nd edn (Cambridge University Press, Cambridge).

Street, B. (1984) *Literacy in Theory and Practice* (Cambridge University Press, Cambridge).

Stubbs, M. (1980) *Language and Literacy* (London, Routledge).

Stubbs, M. (1983) *Discourse Analysis* (Blackwell, Oxford).

Stubbs, M. (1986) *Educational Linguistics* (Blackwell, Oxford).

Stubbs, M. (1987) 'An educational theory of (written) language', in T. Bloor and J. Norrish (eds) *Written Language* (British Studies in Applied Linguistics) (Centre for Information on Language Teaching, London).

Stubbs, M. (1989) 'The state of English in the English state: reflections on the Cox Report', *Language and Education* 34, pp. 235–50.

Stubbs, M. (1993) 'Educational language planning in England and Wales: multicultural rhetoric and assimilationist assumptions' in J. Maybin (ed.) *Language and Literacy in Social Practice* (Multilingual Matters, Clevedon), pp.193–214.

Stubbs, M. and Hillier, H. (eds) (1983) *Readings on Language, Schools and Classrooms* (Routledge/Methuen, London).

Sutcliffe, D. (1983) *British Black English* (Blackwell, Oxford).

Sutcliffe, D. and Wong, A. (eds) (1986) *The Language of the Black Experience* (Blackwell, Oxford).

Swan, J. (1992) *Girls, Boys and Language* (Blackwell, Oxford).

Tannen, D. (1988) *Talking Voices* (Cambridge University Press, Cambridge).

Thomas, G. (1991) *Linguistic Purism* (Longman, London).

Threadgold, T. (1989) 'Talking about genre: ideologies and incompatible discourses', *Cultural Studies* 3 (1), pp. 101–27.

Toolan, M. (1988) *Narrative: A Critical Linguistic Introduction* (Routledge, London).

Trudgill, P. (1975) *Accent, Dialect and the School* (Edward Arnold, London).

Trudgill, P. (1983) *On Dialect* (Blackwell, Oxford).

Trudgill, P. (1984) *Sociolinguistics*, 2nd edn (Penguin, Harmondsworth).

Van Lier, L. (1995) *Introducing Language Awareness* (Penguin, Harmondsworth).

Vygotsky, L. S. (1978) *Mind in Society* (Harvard University Press, Cambridge, Mass.).

Walmsley, J. (1984) *The Uselessness of 'Formal Grammar'?* Working Papers, no. 2, Committee for Linguistics in Education, published by British Association for Applied Linguistics.

Wells, G. (1987) *The Meaning Makers* (Hodder and Stoughton, Sevenoaks).

West, A. (1994) 'The centrality of literature', in S. Brindley (ed.) *Teaching English* (Routledge, London), pp. 124–34.

White, J. (1990) 'On literacy and gender', in R. A. Carter (ed.)

Knowledge about Language and the Curriculum (Hodder and Stoughton, Sevenoaks), pp. 181–96.

Widdowson, H. G. (1989) *Aspects of Language Teaching* (Oxford University Press, Oxford).

Widdowson, H.G. (1990) 'Languages in the National Curriculum', mimeo, University of London, Institute of Education.

Widdowson, H. G. (1992) *Practical Stylistics* (Oxford University Press, Oxford).

Wilkinson, J. (1995) *Introducing Standard English* (Penguin, Harmondsworth).

Williams, R (1983) *Keywords*, 2nd edn (Fontana, London).

Woods, E. (1995) *Introducing Grammar* (Penguin, Harmondsworth).

Wright, T. (1994) *Investigating English* (Edward Arnold, London).